CREATED OR CONSTRUCTED?
The Great Gender Debate

CREATED OR CONSTRUCTED?
The Great Gender Debate

Elaine Storkey

paternoster press

Copyright © 2000 by Elaine Storkey

First published in 2000 by Paternoster Press

Reprinted 2001

07 06 05 04 03 02 01   8 7 6 5 4 3 2

Paternoster Press is an imprint of Paternoster Publishing,
P.O. Box 300, Carlisle, Cumbria, CA3 0QS, UK
http://www.paternoster-publishing.com

British Library Cataloguing in Publication Data
A catalogue record for this book is available from the British Library

ISBN 0-85364-983-9

Cover Design by Mainstream, Lancaster
Typeset by WestKey Limited, Falmouth, Cornwall
Printed in the UK by Biddles Ltd, Guildford, Surrey

Contents

Preface

In what ways are women and men really different, and where do these differences originate? These are probably two of the most common questions I have been asked over the years that I have been researching and lecturing in this area. It seems important to many people that they have a way of finding out. For if our differences are 'fixed' – part of our very biology (irrespective of whether they see that biology as the last point in a process of evolution or given by a Creator) there is little we can do to alter them. We then have to find a way of living with these differences creatively and in a way that produces minimum upset to the good ordering of our relationships. If however they are not fixed, but are part of the shifts and changes in human fashion and social ideas, then it is important that we understand the pressures which shape the patterns of gender difference we observe. We need also to face whether we should be actively reshaping our relationships and, indeed, even restructuring our society into something which offers more wholeness to men and women.

This book takes us through those questions and the various answers that have been offered. It tries to present the arguments as cogently as possible, but using a framework which makes the material easier to follow. Each chapter continues the debate into a new area as the various strands of the discussion are all identified. I look at issues in psychology, sociology, philosophy and in theology. I have my own ideas in each of these areas, of course, which is why I have written the book. But I have tried to present the ideas of others as faithfully as I have presented my own.

What is offered here is an edited and expanded form of the lectures delivered to New College, University of New South Wales in October 1997. In my writing I have taken into consideration many of the questions which my audience at New College posed to me at that occasion and, not surprisingly, these have triggered off more enquiries of my own. It has not been easy to write the lectures up for publication for in this area the debate moves fast and since the lectures were given there have been a number of new key studies. So I have tried to incorporate new arguments and insights published since my visit to the University of New South Wales. I have also taken on board a particular point raised by one woman after the lecture on gender differences in popular psychology. She commented that, although absorbing and entertaining, my lecture had not given her the critical analysis she was hoping for. I have worked hard to remedy that, and hope that Chapter Five will satisfy her request.

A revision of this extent means, however, that those who attended the lectures might find this account of them very different. They will miss the cartoons, the illustrations and probably the jokes. Inevitably, lectures delivered to a group of colleagues and friends in the intimacy of a friendly academic setting is different from a publication which tries to speak to a scattered audience fifty times the size. But I hope they think the finished product is an improvement and one which they are unashamed to hand around to their friends.

Some of the material in this book has a longer history than the New College Lectures, beginning life as notes for the London Lectures in Contemporary Christianity which I delivered in London in 1993. This formed the basis of subsequent study, as did unfinished work left over from my book *The Search For Intimacy* published in 1994. With the publication that has now resulted I feel that I have produced something that has been in gestation state for most of a decade, but which now addresses the current gender debate. Readers who are already familiar with the debate will find the material here complete in itself. Those who are less familiar will be helped by reading my first book, *What's Right With Feminism*. Published originally in 1985 and reprinted many times it will follow this in a new edition updated for the millenium.

Acknowledgements

As always there are key people to thank. I am grateful to the invitation to deliver these lectures which was given by the Master of New College, Dr Allan Beavis. His hospitality, and that of the college as a whole, was rich and warm. I am in debt to Bishop John Reid who first approached me with the idea, and to the New College Lectures Committee who approved it. Fuzz and Carolyn Kitto of the Uniting Church in New South Wales were as hospitable as always and gave me practical and emotional support. My former study assistant, Deborah Halling, and some of my graduate students at King's College, London – Celia McDonald, Clara Swinson, and Christina Rees – have all sent material in my direction, as have Peter Oliver and Janet West in Sydney. Huw Spanner and Brian Draper of *Third Way* kept plying me with relevant books to consider (and of course to review!) as my own took shape. I am grateful to Pieter Kwant and Robin Derricourt for seeing the manuscript through to publication and to Sue Beresford, my colleague and personal/research assistant whose able help has been much valued. Two colleagues at King's have been entirely supportive, Doug Campbell and Alan Torrance (now Professor of Divinty at St Andrew's University, Scotland). Their own scholarship in theology has never ducked the issues raised by others I refer to in this book. Finally, my husband, Alan, once again demonstrated that his commitment to gender equality is practical, not just romantic! He put up with my absences in Australia as I delivered the lectures, and my inaccessibility in the home as I worked on the manuscript. To him and to everyone I offer grateful thanks.

Chapter One

History Lessons

For those who like order, predictability and a settled way of doing things, the 1950s now seem like a period of unparallelled bliss. The war had ended and an optimism had settled over Europe and those of European descent. Fascism had been wiped out; communism seemed for the moment to be at bay and good had triumphed over evil. Of course there were things to be sorted out. The full extent of the atrocities was still dawning. I came upon a report written in 1945 by the allied inspectors at Buchenwald, the Jewish extermination camp. It makes chilling reading, for there was much they simply did not know. They documented the horrors (trenches full of corpses, and furniture and lampshades in the Commandant's house made from human skin) but said they had no evidence of any actual torture, and the Jewish survivors told them of camps they believed were worse. The inspectors reported simply, 'The name of Auschwitz occurred several times.'

By the 1950s we knew all about Auschwitz and much more. There was little counselling for either the returned war veterans, or for the devastated Jewish community, so many of whom had seen their families decimated. All the men and women damaged by the war had simply to put it behind them, and plan for the future. The world was committed to peace, to prosperity, to rebuilding for the future and to change. In Britain, the search for a new start drew many whole families away from their slowly recovering motherland. They sailed out to Canada and the other Commonwealth countries, but most travelled to Australia and New Zealand. Here, they began a different life with different challenges, yet content for the next few decades to be joined with Britain under its new young monarch who had succeeded to the throne. Back in England, my parents' generation rebuilt our country and tried, like people throughout Europe and North America, to return to normality. There was optimism, the end of rationing, jobs for everyone, and a massive reconstruction problem to tackle: the rebuilding of lives, cities, the economy, schools, universities and families.

The problem was, however, that it was never that simple. For the war had unsettled relationships, patterns of hierarchy and values, and the 1950s ultimately failed to win the new generation over to the perspectives of the old. Things were changing at the very heart of these societies. One key change was the whole area of how men and women were to relate to each other in the varied areas of their lives. Issues of sex and gender began to surface in the areas of work, education, and in the family, and a challenge began to be mounted which many in society did not understand. Why could things not stay as they were? But as they were, when? For there were historical variants in the relationships between men and women, and in so many ways, this new half-century was to be quite unlike anything that had gone before. Who was to say which of the historical lessons needed to be called upon in the years following the 1950s?

Analysing the past was not, however, the usual method chosen for sorting out issues of sex and gender. For, strange though it might now seem, people in the 1950s were largely unaware of gender history. Most of it was not written up until over a decade later. The relevant stories in that history had not been the focus of university research, or programmes of teaching. Memories were tossed around in folklore or old family archives but were not fully recorded and studied in public places. Even recent gender history – say that of Britain in the nineteenth century – was often inaccessible, unless people went out to look for it. Many fascinating accounts of why many women came to Australia and New Zealand from the 1800s onwards had to wait two more decades before excited students of history finally wrote them up.[1]

---

[1] See, for example, H. Heney, *Australia's Founding Mothers* (Sydney: Nelson, 1978); J.A Hone 'The Movement for the Higher

The Nineteenth Century's 'Superfluous Women'

This absence of analysis is curious because, even though it had rarely been articulated self-consciously in history books, Britain had struggled with the gender issue over and over again. Much of it had been in the nineteenth century which, for people in the 1950s was still recent or even living memory. One of the problems then had been that of the 'superflous woman'. In the 1860s and again in the 1880s, for example, very many men had been killed in wars leaving an inbalance in the adult population. Demographic factors added to this as the infant mortality rate was higher amongst young male infants. Consequently for much of the latter part of the nineteenth century there was an acute problem of too few men and too many women in the British population.

How did we get to know this? Not through being taught it in 1950s school history classes, but through the legacy of party games. The Victorians had an intriguing card game 'Old Maid'. It was a game which involved collecting cards of family members: Mother/Father/Son/Daughter and so on, until you had a full set. But also in the pack was the one card nobody wanted, namely the 'Old Maid'. The point of the game was to use any amount of ingenuity or deceit to get rid of the Old Maid from your hand of acceptable family relations and palm her off on to someone else. In humorous, yet cruel, detail the game echoed the problem of the 'superfluous woman' in British society. An unmarried middle-class woman was a liability. Working-class women could go into domestic service or factory work, but those too highly bred for such labour were always someone's dependant: a father's, uncle's, or brother's.

So the solution was to marry her off, send her out as a governess or companion to an elderly widow, encourage her into the newly revitalised religious orders, or ship her out to the

---

[1] *(continued)* Education of Women in Victoria in the later nineteenth century', MA thesis, (Monash, 1966). One exception is the biography of the pioneering Australian woman, *Caroline Chisholm* by M. Kiddle (Melbourne: Melbourne University Press, 1950).

colonies; and hundreds of unmarried ladies crossed the oceans. The English Gentlewoman's Emigration Society, founded by an Anglican clergyman, offered a more protected passage for single travellers, and provided spunky middle-class women as wives for the farmers and workers of Australia and New Zealand, where there was still a woman shortage. The very first settlement at Botany Bay had been overwhelmingly male. Out of 725 convicts there were only 192 women. Half a century later men still predominated.

Once they were there of course, women worked. Gentlewomen who, in Britain, would have been barely able to move across the room, so tightly were they laced in their 'waspies', were hacking into the native bush, working as ranchers' wives or travelling long distances on horseback. Some thrived on the change and discovered a freedom of space and basic lifestyle completely unavailable to them in Britain. Yet for others it cannot have been an easy life especially when expatriate gentlewomen were an oddity in the society. As Janet West remarks in her excellent study, the cult of machismo in Australia is 'probably a descendent of the early colonial days of womanlessness'.[2] How the emigrant women coped is a major study of its own.

Education and Missionary Work

The nineteenth century had also marked the beginning of changes in other areas of women's lives. Education held the key. In every era of European history there had been those parents who had believed that an educated woman is a better companion than an uneducated one, and had provided tutors for their daughters. But women's education became public policy in the nineteenth century, extending into higher education. In 1878 the University of London opened degrees to women, and by the turn of the century women were accepted

---

[2] Janet West, *Daughters of Freedom: A History of Women in the Australian Church* (Sydney: Albatross Books, 1997) p. 22. See also her comment on the emigrant clergy daughter, Rachel Henning, p. 23.

as at least a peripheral part of the undergraduate world. In 1897 the Women's Institute produced a listing of women at each university in Britain. The nine women's colleges of Cambridge, Oxford and London universities had a total of 778 students, the largest number (192) being admitted to Bedford College, London, which had been opened in 1849. Girton in Cambridge, (initially known as Hitchin College) founded in 1869, was the first women's residential college; and the London residential college, Westfield, founded on Evangelical Church of England principles with bible study at the centre of its curriculum, now had 44 women on its list.[3]

In Australia a similar pattern had followed. Compulsory education for both sexes had been introduced from 1866 onwards. Victoria implemented this in 1874, South Australia in 1875, and New South Wales in 1880. The University of Adelaide was opened in 1872 and allowed women to attend lectures from the start, but they could not receive degrees until 1880. It took nine years of planning and negotiation before Melbourne opened its university to women, and that was not until Sydney University had declared the principle of women's rights and equality in 1888.[4]

By the beginning of the twentieth century, the possibility of education and professional employment for women was beginning to look like an attractive alternative to economic dependence on male relatives. For some women it was an attractive alternative even to marriage.

Christian women benefited vocationally, at least in principle, for they could now be equipped educationally for the outreach work of the gospel which had been absorbing women's talents for some years already. Yet this principle did not extend of course to preaching and ministering in Britain.

---

[3] C.S. Bremer, 'Women in the British Universities', Appendix A of Mrs Henry Sidwick, *The Place of University Education in the Life of Women* (London: Transactions of the Women's Insitute, 1897) pp. 34–52. See also Martha Vicinus, *Independent Women, Work and Community for Single Women 1850-1920* (London: Virago, 1985) Chapter 4, pp. 121–162.

[4] West, *Daughters*, p. 31.

To follow a calling to evangelise, Christian women had to travel overseas. And travel they did, throughout the nineteenth century, and on journeys that sometimes took weeks. Unlike many other women they were not going in order to find basic employment or someone to marry, but to give their lives to missionary activity in far distant lands. Not surprisingly, from the start, overseas missions made great use of women. The Society for Promoting Female Education in the Far East had begun in the late 1820s, and early missionaries set up five schools in Malacca. In India, the Zenana Bible and Medical Mission, founded in the 1850s, was a women's mission for over a hundred years before admitting men as members in 1952. 1877 marked a turning point for women missionaries in China as a famine in Shansi province claimed the lives of nine to thirteen million people, and opened doors to western women to come to work and minister to those who survived.[5] Mary Lawry was the first missionary born in Australia to serve overseas. She went out from Parramatta with her English-born husband to Tonga and worked with the Tongans on their own ground, visiting them in their homes. (Her ministry was markedly more successful than her husband's but this did not stop the *Wesleyan Methodist Magazine* from editing her name out of her husband's accounts of their work in Tonga.)[6]

Whether in Calabar, or in the Crimea, much of this early work was undertaken in uncharted territory where few westerners had ever been before. And it was carried out often without back-up from organised agencies who could offer support and sometimes protection. Long before the later missionary societies had devised programmes of preparation for overseas missionary work, these early women learnt the local language and customs for themselves, and gave a lifetime of service to cultures they had made their own. How they coped with homesickness and frustration is the subject of many poignant biographies.

---

[5] See the work of Valerie Griffiths on women in missionary activity. See also her chapter in Kathy Keay (ed.), *Men, Women and God* (London: Marshall Pickering, 1996) pp. 61–77.
[6] As cited by Margaret Reason, *Currency Lass* (Sydney, Albatross 1985) p. 227.

Suffrage

The suffrage campaigns were also very significant. Both New Zealand and Australia made much earlier progress than Britain. In New Zealand in 1893, thirteen years after young women had received the right to a tertiary education in the country's universities, they were given the right to vote. This was not without opposition of course. The campaigners had been parodied as the 'shrieking sisterhood'. A year later, in 1894, women were given the vote in South Australia. The Woman's Suffrage League had persuaded almost one third of the colony's adult population to sign a petition calling for universal suffrage. South Australia also became the first place in the world to allow women to stand for the legislature. In America women had to wait until 1920 before they could vote in federal elections, and it took Britain until 1928 to grant suffrage to all women over twenty one.

The suffrage campaign in Britain, however, had undoubtedly been held up by the First World War whose aftermath brought another massive demographic problem. Thousands of women lost their husbands, fiancés and sweethearts and were never to marry again. It is no coincidence that the 1920s in Britain saw an upsurge in spiritualist interest among women as they tried to contact the dead. But, more usefully, it also saw the burgeoning of new openings for women in the professions. Certainly, women were now educated for these roles, but there was also the necessity of ordering a society in a way which did not require equal numbers of marriageable men and women in the population. Consequently, the growth in women's education, the opening up of the professions and the acceptance that a single woman no longer had to be economically dependent on her male relatives all brought an excess of women into areas of work which had previously been the sole preserve of men. Hardy women professionals created a new tradition alongside the old-boy networks and passed on their skills to younger women. By the outbreak of the Second World War women knew what would be expected of them. Many of them were ready to move into the areas of the economic planning and production vacated by the men at the front.

Back in the Fifties

So, long before the 1950s, the gender issue had surfaced again and again. Yet these cameos of recent history, let alone the many different nuances of gender changes throughout the centuries in the West, were somehow forgotten in the 1950s. The post-war years were a period of unparalled 'traditionalism'. The men demobbed from the armed forces needed work, countries needed children, and families needed mothers. It was a time when stability was prized almost above all else. In Britain, although less so in the United States, the return to domesticity went largely uncontested. Being allowed to be homemakers, and continue as homemakers long after children had left home, was experienced as liberation for those who had been required to go out to work during the war. The emphasis on the male breadwinner was reinforced by the media, by schools, and by public policies. Education programmes made some nod towards the need to equip women for dual careers of motherhood and work, but by and large, work was seen along strong lines of gender demarcation. Gender history was put on hold, and those who were Christianly inclined saw those roles as laid down by God.

Yet the *status quo* would not hold for long. The assumption that there was an unbroken line of fixed sex and gender roles from the garden of Eden to the middle of the twentieth century was soon going to be shattered. A new generation that had not embraced the need for sacrifice for King and Country was going to call into question all that the fifties stood for. It was going to challenge politics, economics, sexuality, education, and morality. It was going to challenge the traditions of its forebears as simply 'conservative ideology', and one of the most turbulent debates was going to be that of sex and gender.

Pre-modern, Modern and Postmodern

I have chosen to position my comments round the 1950s because that period is now sometimes regarded as the last era where public attitudes were consensual and largely 'pre-modern'. Several contemporary writers use a classification which distinguishes between the pre-modern, modern and postmodern,[7] and I want to borrow those categories now. I do so, however, recognizing that they are not very precise analytical tools. There are no specific epochs or dates to which these terms refer as they are not historical groupings. Nor do they describe social movements or rigorous intellectual schools of thought. They are more nebulous: concepts which relate to cultural demarcations, mind-sets, attitudes, value-systems. The 'pre-modern', which embraces many of the attitudes widespread in the 1950s, is about predictability and tradition and is markedly different from the 'modern' and its questioning of ideology and identifying hidden assumptions. With its emphasis on competing explanations and consciousness-raising, the modern challenged the pre-modern but replaced traditional values with an ideology of its own which, in turn, has been rejected. Since the mid-1980s we have been moving into the 'postmodern', which recognizes, most of all, the fluidity of relationships, the plurality of cultures, the diversity of people groups, the dethroning of the West and western ideology, and the relativism of meanings. Of course it is in the very nature of postmodernity that it does not exist on its own. In our postmodern society there will be very many (often the majority) who are still pre-modern and modern. But culturally their voice will be muted and their relevance often dismissed because they belong to another era: something more fixed, more definite, appealing to a metanarrative.

In working with these demarcations I recognize that my comments will be provisional, but that is in keeping with the postmodern, for in postmodernity there are few endings and no fixed points of reference. Yet my own analysis is not a postmodern one. It is one which recognizes the importance of 'deconstruction' and yet also acknowledges that we can only deconstruct from a particular location. My own location will become evident as the chapters unfold.

---

[7] Jean Joseph Goux, 'Irigaray vs the Utopia of the Neutral Sex' in C. Burke, N. Schor and M. Whiford (eds.), *Engaging with Irigaray* (New York: Columbia University Press, 1994) p. 189.

Although I have said that the 1950s are regarded as the last era when public attitudes were pre-modern, this does not mean that pre-modernity no longer exists except amongst individual people. In fact, with regard to the relationship between men and women, those attitudes have continued to exist in substantial pockets of society even though there have been many other changes in the way we see things. The very question of this book, whether as human beings (male and female) we are 'created or constructed', is not one that has been settled during any period. The debate has been continuous. Even when the overall cultural response has gone in one direction, there have always been substantial influential minorities which have taken up a different answer. What I now want to do is to read the debate about sex and gender relations through the demarcations of pre-modern, modern and postmodern and I believe that what sounds provisional at the outset will be much firmer by the conclusion.

Chapter Two

The Pre-modern in Sex and Gender

When I decided to borrow the concepts of pre-modern, modern and postmodern I inherited a problem. Whose definition do I use? In fact the answer is pre-decided. For these concepts are those already developed by postmodern writers. That means that the pre-modern, for example, does not actually exist except as a category offered to us by postmodernity. So, to use these terms at all means I have initially to allow the postmodern definitions to prevail. What follows in this chapter is therefore an analysis already filtered through a certain value framework. I shall reappraise this later, but meanwhile readers can assess for themselves to what extent the analysis holds weight.

According to Goux the pre-modern is characterised by fixed order, fixed roles, and fixed explanations, reinforced by accepted tradition. At its heart lies an essentialism: the idea that a certain 'essence' defines the centre of our identity as human beings, and as men and women. In gender terms this means there is a firm belief that men have certain identifiable, fixed characteristics and women have other identifiable, fixed characteristics, and that these identifiers are rooted in our very nature. Whether this is backed by careful analysis or serious scholarship has not mattered until recently. The appeal has always been to what is supposedly obvious and needs no explanation.

Pre-modern thinking about gender relations, if indeed it can be given the label 'thinking', was therefore largely at the level of assumption rather than analysis or examination. Attitudes about men and women, epitomised in the 1950s, were widely held but rarely scrutinised or reflected on. Even so, these attitudes undergirded so much of society. They were reflected in family patterns, work roles, social policy and curriculum development. They were reinforced by advertising, films and romantic novels. Men were always tall, strong, direct and authoritative; women were always passive, responsive, attractive and young. The romantic Hollywood fantasy was that the ultimate success of a woman was in transforming one of these gloriously single-minded male creatures into a hopelessly lovelorn suitor who thought of little else but her.

The gender attitudes of pre-modernity became 'normalised' in the minds of those who expressed them. These attitudes defined reality and it took another era to identify them as ideological. Well-worn clichés, strings of 'truisms' justified most social practices, if indeed any justification was deemed necessary. A woman's place was in the home, women were intuitive, nurturant, passive, instinctual, emotional, good with their hands, but easily distracted. As 'weaker vessels' women needed to be protected, often from themselves and their own irrationality. Men were the ones to whom this task of leadership and protection automatically fell. They were strong, protective, hardy, analytical, objective and more single-minded. Men were best suited to lead, women to follow. Men, with their greater rational, objective capacity, could more readily detach themselves from emotional situations, whereas women were too easily influenced by their feelings.

The societies which were built on these attitudes were inevitably ones which prized and rewarded all those characteristics that were seen as male: toughness, inflexibility, hard bargaining, single-minded vision, uncompromising firmness, confrontation with opponents and defeating the opposition. Not surprisingly, in this masculine-constructed reality (what the later feminists were going to call patriarchy) those men who found themselves ill at ease with these stereotypes courted disapproval and felt excluded. In fact, the only way real men could express love for each other was either in the 'tough ways' of Australian machismo-insults, thumping, practical jokes, heavy drinking and general bawdiness, or in the restrained stiff-upper-lip emotions of the English officer class. There, true depth of feeling was barely betrayed by language:

'I just want to say sir, you are a very decent chap, and I would give my life for you.' Whilst the women were given permission to express a wide range of passions to each other, the men struggled to find their own language of feelings within emotionally repressive cultures. The message conveyed, subtly but unmistakably, was that for men to display any emotion, other than loyalty, pride at achievement, competitiveness, anger, or controlled lust was unmanly. And if in their relationship with women the control was not always there, that was also understandable.

How did the pre-modern mind justify its stereotypes? Almost always by an appeal to what they called the 'natural', usually identified as biological and frequently as God-given. Human attributes were all created, or, for those who had no time for a Creator, they evolved. Male and female characteristics were fixed, rooted in nature, in biology. They were givens, indelible, non-negotiable imperatives and formed the basis for all human authority structures. The forces of biology were definitive and unchanging. For either sex to move away from its given characteristics and adopt those which pertained to the opposite sex was alarming. Such a move went against nature. Certain branches of the church claimed to find a reinforcement of this essentialism in biblical teaching, insisting that it is implied in the very order of creation. For, since nature was created by God, and since it was God's idea to have male and female, the blurring of sexual distinctives transgressed the very will of God. Something that was called 'natural order' or 'tradition as divinely ordained' had to be fiercely upheld.

The French writer Fénelon expressed in 1721 what many pre-moderns were to maintain for the next two and a half centuries: 'To violate the rights of established subordination is . . . to blaspheme against Providence, and threaten the rights of the sovereign father and head of the family who gives to each of his children his allotted place.'[1] To alter established gender roles was nothing less than to desex

---

[1] Fénelon, *Essai philosophique sur le gouvernement civil* (1921), quoted in Jean Joseph Goux, 'Irigaray', p. 178.

humanity. As we shall see later, these attitudes were going to be still evident in the 1990s in the Church of England debate on the ordination of women.

What became evident is that for those who thought in a pre-modern way the sex-gender dichotomy did not exist. There was no difference between sex and gender, for all was decided by sex. Biology provided the essentialism which delivered the structure of all human roles and relationships. The idea that there were cultural reasons for the way men and women functioned was not seriously considered. The splitting apart of sex as a biological category and gender as a cultural category had to wait until the 'moderns' began their critique.

The main problem with the pre-modern position is now well recognized. It rests on a biological determinism which reduces all the complexity of human relationships to basic genetic or anatomic categories. Yet pre-modern assumptions have never disappeared from the gender debate and indeed they have been making something of a comeback in recent years. Because of this, and indeed as a matter of common courtesy, we need to pay some attention to the arguments that are given for placing so much weight on biology. And we need to examine too the anxieties about changing roles which are often evident amongst traditionalists, including Christians, who hold this position.

The Evidence from Biology

It would be foolish to deny that biology does play a key part in human relationships and sexual differentiation. Men and women are not only sexually different, they are different chromosomally, reproductively, anatomically, hormonally and in terms of weight, height and brain usage. Figures quoted suggest that men are, on average, 7 per cent taller and 20 per cent heavier than women. The very categories – male and female – are *sexual* categories, and we experience much of our identity through our sexuality. What is more, pre-modern notions about what is natural did not emerge from nowhere. They were often reinforced by research from psychologists or biologists.

Studies on the effects of an 'explosion of testosterone' in aggressive behaviour in male rats, for example, may be dated and rather dubious when applied directly to male humans, but clearly there is something there which needs to be taken into consideration. Similarly, although far too much has been laid at the door of 'pre-menstrual tension' it has some significance. Women's mood swings and attitudes to events, work or relationships are not dissociated from their biological cycle.

Longevity

The differences between men and women express themselves in other very evident ways. Of the current population in Britain 1.1 million people live to be over 85 years of age. But at age 89 there are three women to every man. The conclusion is unavoidable. Put simply, it is that women last longer. And this is in spite of childbearing, and the increase of invasive cancers amongst women. Some argue that they face fewer hazards than men. Yet studies on survival rates amongst comparative males and females suggest there are other factors. An interesting piece of research was done some years ago on 40,000 monks and nuns. This was a very useful comparative sample for the subjects were all free from the perils of dangerous occupations and the stresses and often emotional trauma of family lives. They were all non-smoking teetotalers. If any group could be expected to show a similarity in life expectation it should be this one. Yet the study established that by the age of forty-five the nuns could expect to live five and a half years longer than the monks![2]

Sexual Disorders

The influence of biology comes out even more strongly when we look at the effects of sexual disorders in men and women. For example the disorder 'S alpha – reductese deficiency' (an

[2] Quoted in Roger Hurding, 'Restoring the Image' in K. Keay (ed.), *Men, Women and God* (London: Marshall Pickering, 1986) p. 293.

enzyme deficiency) – results in genetic males being born with genitalia of female appearance. So there is an ambiguity about sexuality until puberty, when, with the usual surge of testosterone, masculinity occurs – the voice deepens and the phallus enlarges. Problems of coping with the disorder are often compounded because many of these young men will have previously been raised as girls. Whatever problems of sexual identity these particular young people have already encountered will be much greater after puberty as they now have to learn the behaviour, patterns and attitudes of men. The counter disorder in women – congenital adrenal hyperplasia – is a genetically recessive condition that leads to vinilisation of females, i.e. genetically female children are born with masculinised genitalia with again a resultant confusion of identity. There is also some evidence of an increased incidence of lesbianism in women with this disorder. The conclusions from these observations are that biology is a powerful determinant of our identity, and when biology sends ambiguous messages, people are thrown into confusion.

Brain Hemispheres

Yet however significant hormonal influence or sexual disorders may be (and they are obviously very signficant in the lives of those who have to work through them) too much weight can be placed on making these the overall argument about gender. That is why some others who argue for biology make their case, more enthusiastically, from research done on male-female brains, and the contrasting usage by men and women of different brain hemispheres. A number of claims have been made. 'The difference between the male and female brain is now well attested by different researchers. Women have stronger connections between the two halves of their brains, men have stronger connections within each half of the brain.' Or, put another way, 'Women have the skills to win the Nobel Peace Prize, but it is a rare woman who will win the Nobel Prize for Physics or for Economics, and that has nothing to do with society's bias, but all to do with the male's inbuilt advantage. He simply finds higher or abstract mathematics easier.'[3] Some have used this to suggest it is not only inefficient and wasteful to train women to think 'like men', it might also be harmful.

Sociobiology

It is interesting that in all of these areas there has been a comfortable alliance between those who hold a position where a natural order is established by biology and pre-moderns whose starting point is Christianity. I shall focus more on this later, but want to say here that Christians who believe that different sex roles are willed by God and reinforced by Scripture are pleased to see their ideas given some 'scientific' weight. Yet although they find many of these theories relatively benign, there are others which are clearly problematic. Christians with 'biologistic' sympathies do not know what to make of sociobiology for example. On the one hand it stresses the gulf between male and female more than any other theory. On the other it rests so heavily upon an aggressive evolutionary base, and produces an ethical standpoint which is at best amoral, and at worst the law of the jungle. I have been in lectures where there has been enormous enthusaism for the categorical nature of the assertions, until the implications for moral judgements are pointed out.

Sociobiology attempts to explain the origins of differences between male and female behaviour. It also tries to address what effects biology has on the structuring of societies. Unlike the other research, the focus here is not anatomy, hormones, physiology, or brain hemispheres. It is the *gene*. Through the gene information, traits and characteristics are passed from one generation to the next. The 'selfish gene theory' in effect argues that one of the most basic genetic impulses throughout all species is the desire to reproduce. So we are driven to find the maximal conditions to ensure the survival of *our* genes, even if

---

[3] Anne and Bill Moir, *Why Men Don't Iron: The Real Science of Gender Studies* (London: HarperCollins, 1998) p. 118.

that means the destruction of others. And this gives us the clue to male-female roles and behaviour patterns.

Men and women have different amounts of reproductive material. Men produce sperm in extremely large quantities. Women have eggs in relatively small numbers, and because of the period of gestation not even all of these could produce babies. In theory, then, a man could produce hundreds of off-spring if he could find enough sexual partners and summon up enough energy. Yet if a woman managed to give birth to twenty children she would be doing very well! So at the heart of our difference lies this genetic diversity where men have many more chances than women of reproducing their genes, and, say the sociobiologists, conflict is inevitable, because the needs of each sex are so different. Men need many partners and are geneti-cally driven towards promiscuity and competitveness. Women on the other hand need a protected environment. They need security and the best mate possible to ensure the maximum efficiency and survival of their genes. So their 'drives' are towards exclusiveness and stability. Now, societies do what they can to organize themselves so that these incompatible needs can be best met. But what are seen as societal disorders – rape, male violence – are the spillover of the genetic differences between male and female. These re-emerge spasmodically and inevitably, resisting the social taboos which we have used to restrain them.

Not surprisingly, given all the examples offered above, the tendency to root all differences between women and men ulti-mately in biology (whether seen as created by God or as a product of evolution) has proved powerful. What other source can there be? The onus has been on those who disagree to offer a better explanation.

Problems with these Explanations

Although apparently persuasive, there are problems with each of these explanations. Sociobiology[4] has glaring weaknesses in

---

[4] Richard Dawkins, *The Selfish Gene* (Oxford: OUP, 1976).

that it has no basis for any coherent moral framework. When everything is referred back to the need to procreate, what sexual ethic is possible except, follow your urges? That has made it less attractive to supporters. It is difficult to justify buying into a theory which by implication justifies rape and promiscuity! Other critics point out that it also rests on a variety of concepts which are highly speculative, such as 'genetic predispositions', or 'selfish genes'. How can you ever devise a test for identifying these? The theory also uses a dubious methodology of induction from animal research to human motivation. Yet it is not only sociobiology which is problematic. All of these positions which rest on assumptions about the inevitability of our biology have fundamental flaws. For any reductionism offers a weak theoretical framework. Social, cultural and psychological factors cannot be reduced to biological ones, and these factors have always been complex. Even when we look at incontrovertible evidence from examples of sexual disorder, biology is not the full story. Being told you are a girl, whilst you are born with male genitalia, is also going to cause gender confusion. It will involve one's sense of self, relationship with parents, peers, siblings and members of the opposite sex. Reinforcement of gender attitudes over many years is much more difficult to undo than learning to adopt a different position from which to urinate!

There is also an underlying problem here with definitions. Very often the concepts we use take their meaning in a way that assumes the 'male is norm'. Look at the word 'strength' for example. It usually refers to muscle power, vigour, force, ability to lift weights, and so on. Within this definition the obvious conclusion is that men are stronger than women. They run faster, throw further, hit harder. But if we changed the definition to include stamina, perseverence, or the longevity we noted earlier, we would have a different paradigm. Then, women would be as strong, if not stronger than men since they stay alive longer, and can carry babies within their bodies for nine months. Our definitions do more than just denote difference: they evaluate it along male lines.

How far all these classifications take us is dubious anyway. Take the studies on male-female differences in the way we use our brains. They are full of ambiguities. Roger Sperry, a Nobel prize-winning neuroscientist, has warned against the tendency to over-connect certain abilities to each side of the brain, pointing out how much more the brain works as an integrated whole.[5] Since his own work is on hemispheric specializations that is advice worth heeding. At the safest level of conclusion it would seem that women are more likely to use the parts of their brain which develop linguistic skills, whereas men develop the skills which take them into science or engineering. However, that fact alone does not help us much.

A contemporary researcher suggests that if you translate this into what happens in jobs in society, it would produce a ratio of 3:2 of men to women. That means we could expect 60 per cent of all scientists and engineers to be male and 40 per cent female. But nothing like 40 per cent of scientists and engineers are female. The ratio is much smaller. In fact for the last thirty years more than 90 per cent of engineers have been men. So the findings from research into male and female brains does not explain the disparity that has actually existed. Nor does it explain the other changes today, where girls in the UK are beginning to outstrip boys educationally in most subjects. They have had the edge in many school subjects for several years, but this is increasing to many others. It is also moving up through higher education. In fact, it is now only in physics and engineering that men outstrip women right throughout the system.

So it is not just about biology, for something more than biology is clearly at stake. Nor is it about what is 'natural' because what one society thinks is 'natural', another society can think is highly unnatural. What is missing from the equation is a recognition of the social framework: the location, upbringing, expectations and belief structures that people hold. For it is these which give shape to our ideas about sex and gender, and translate those ideas into action. As we moved out of the first half of the twentieth century, ideas began to change. And the awareness of cultural pressures became important to those thinkers who were about to follow.

---

[5] Quoted in Mary van Leuwan, *Gender and Grace* (Leicester: IVP, 1990) p. 104.

The early post-war period of the 'return to normality' was coming to a close. The optimistic rebuilding of the 1950s and the traditional assumptions about sex were to be shaken by an unprecedented storm of radicalism in the 1960s. Modernist analyses of gender were about to attack pre-modernity at its very foundations and frame out a new structure on the edifice of the old. In particular, the assumptions about the limitations of biology were going to be seen in the light of political and social constructions. Education, equal pay legislation and a shift in the composition of the workforce would force a tense rethinking. The debate about male and female was about to enter a dramatic new phase.

Chapter Three

Modernism and Gender Relationships

It is somewhat banal to refer to the social theorists writing in the 1960s and 1970s simply as 'modernists'. Theirs were complex arguments, and there were many differences and disagreements between them. But the use of the concept 'modernist' by the postmodern writer, Jean Joseph Goux, is simply to denote the middle point of a journey between pre-modernity and postmodernity.[1] From my point of view I want to present them as moving us from the 'creation' to the 'construction' side of the gender debate. In Goux's analysis, they did this because their central concern was a rebellion against biological essentialism.

This rebellion took a variety of forms. The first rebels, the early feminists of the 1960s, accepted that biological factors divided women and men, but rejected the consequences. They identified women's anatomical and reproductive differences from men as the crucial problem. These differences meant that women were trapped in limiting lifestyles and made dependent upon men. Their slogan 'biology is destiny' became, in effect, a rallying cry encouraging women to refuse to give in to the future which their sexuality mapped out for them. Biology must not be allowed to be destiny. So new ideas for limiting the effects of sexual differences and especially the force of the women's reproductive role were put forward.

Two of the most widespread demands were placarded at every demonstration and on every piece of publicity. They were for legalised abortion and twenty-four-hour nursery care.

---

[1] See Goux, 'Irigaray' p. 189.

Abortion in particular was regarded as a central plank of women's liberation. Those advocating it felt it would free them from having to continue with unwanted pregnancies and give them choice about what to do with their own bodies. No one else had the moral right to tell women what they should do. Yet even after the Abortion Reform Law was passed the campaigning continued because the requirements laid down by the law still fell short of abortion on demand, and women were still not free to make the decision entirely for themselves. Other people were involved in the approval for the abortion process, and many restrictions remained in place. That remains the legal position today, and, with some caveats, rightly so. Abortion is a profoundly social and moral issue, not simply a matter of individual choice of whether or not to allow a pregnancy to result in childbirth. The very least the law can do is offer some safeguards, both for women and their children.

Safeguards were not uppermost in the minds of these earlier writers. There were other suggestions that went even further in the attempt to even out the biological imbalances between women and men. Some argued that legalised abortion had as its focus the 'masculisation' of women. The aim of the abortion-on-demand lobby was to enable women to make the sorts of decisions which were only available to those who did not have to carry babies, i.e. men. But we could also argue that other, more radical, measures had as their focus the 'feminisation' of men as the aim of the 'biological manipulation' lobby was to move towards the effective eradication of difference. The idea here was that rather than leave women to endure the effects of their biology alone, men should be encouraged to share it. In particular, men should be galvanized to share the physical childbearing which had penalised women and restricted their freedom in the world of work. This could be done if a temporary substitute womb could be produced in the male body by surgically adapting the bladder.[2] This 'womb' could then carry an embryo fathered by the man and transplanted from his partner, and this temporary home

---

[2] See Shulamith Firestone, *The Dialectic of Sex: The Case for a Feminist Revolution* (London: Jonathon Cape, 1971).

would take the embryo through to full term. The suggestion was made with enthusiasm and widely discussed (along with ideas for freeing women by transplanting the human embryo into the uterus of a large mammal). Yet it was not taken seriously by more than a handful of people and was more widely regarded as just science fiction. It had to wait another twenty years for the *New Scientist* to hail it as a medical possibility.[3]

But something else was changing, not just a scepticism about the workability of particular suggestions. There was a growing unease from within feminism about what was being surrendered by this kind of response to essentialism. All these suggestions addressed the apparent symptoms and tried, in some way or another, to change the impact of biology. But not one of them delved beneath the symptoms to make sure they had their diagnosis right. In fact, they left the underlying assumptions of pre-modernity intact: biology stayed the focus of the issue. These writers did not challenge the implicit notion that the fundamental definition of woman was a biological one, they simply brought forward proposals to ameliorate its effects.

Biology is not Destiny

There had to be another way of rebelling against biological essentialism. And that way was, quite simply, to reject its claims. A new group of writers did that. They argued that biology was 'itself part of the ideology of gender inequality, rather than an independent authority which can offer neutral arbitration on the "facts".'[4] The new modernist writers therefore refused to buy into the old perspective and set to work mounting a critique of its assumptions. They worked from alternative presuppositions and with an alternative commitment. Biology did not provide any framework for

---

[3] New Scientist 'Male pregnancy "achievable soon"', *The Times*, 24 May 1984.

[4] Elaine Graham, *Making the Difference: Gender, Personhood and Theology* (London: Mowbray, 1995) p. 94.

understanding what was essential in human relationships. In fact, if anything was seen to be essential in the relation between male and female, it was a common humanity, and that highlighted the need for mutual justice and equality.

The new perspective moved away from biological reductionism, and once old assumptions about the primacy of biology were discarded, all kinds of new possibilities were opened up. Instead of being hung up on their differences, we could look at *similarities* between women and men. For men and women are really quite alike. They reflect one another in all kinds of characteristics, capabilities, intellect or stamina. Men organise, women organise; women teach, men teach; men heal the sick, women heal the sick. It was simply that women in the past had not been given the chance to develop their assets as fully and freely as they could. But once they did, and women were given equality in law, education and training, they would have access to roles usually occupied by men. Then we would see the gender-segregated structure of society beginning to collapse.

The Journey from Sex to Gender

So the new rebellion finally departed fundamentally and decisively from pre-modernity. There were two key ideas which had to be rejected. The first was the the notion of the 'natural' which had to be replaced very thoroughly with the 'social'. The argument here was clear, human beings are socially constructed, not biologically created. Being a human person is not just about instincts or drives, that would be animal behaviour. But as humans we think and act. We are as much products of social change as of any biological evolution. So much so, in fact, that any differences can only be clearly understood when they are seen in their social location. So behind all ethnic, sexual or class divergences are social, economic and political factors. Issues that surround ethnicity are not about differences in skin pigmentation but about income, privilege, customs, dress, religion, language, access to work and so on. Similarly, comparisons between women and men must be made against the backcloth of attitudes, access, expectations and control rather than focusing on their reproductive differences. As one writer observed, 'If race, sex and class were not politically and economically significant categories, it is likely that no one would care very much about biological differences between members of these groups.'[5] So, in modernity, the interest shifted from the genetic, reproductive and physiological differences of biology to the way society was structured, and the roles which resulted. Addressing those factors would be the key to change.

The second was therefore a rejection of the over-simplified idea of *sex* for the complex notion of *gender*. For sex, male and female is obviously not an adequate category for understanding the complexities of man-woman relationships. For so much of what occurs in those relationships is not about sex but about gender, being masculine or feminine. These are, again, related to culture, nurture, expectations and social traditions. Germaine Greer explains, 'Masculinity is to maleness as femininity is to femaleness. That is to say that maleness is the natural condition, the sex if you like, and masculinity is the cultural constuct, the gender.'[6] Being a man and a woman is as much about *learning* to be masculine and feminine as it is about living with ones differences in chromosones. People in different cultures learn different ways of being masculine and feminine, men and women, according to the attitudes and expectations which are prevalant. Most of the problems in social relationships are not caused by any biological differences between male and female: they are caused by what society does *with* those differences.

So the modernists were challenging both the reductionism of the pre-modern mind, and its espousal of biology as an explanatory framework. With the changing of the discourse,

---

[5] M. Lowe, 'Sociobiology and Sex Differences', *Signs: Journal of Women in Culture and Society*, 4 (1978) p. 55 or, 'The Dialectic of Biology and Culture' in M. Lowe and R. Hubbard (eds.), *Women's Nature: Rationalizations of Inequality* (Oxford: Pergamon Press, 1983) p. 55.

[6] Germaine Greer, *The Whole Woman* (London/Auckland: Doubleday, 1999) p. 288.

the old arguments about the biological differences between male or female were left behind, and a new appraisal of how the culture interprets and presents the differences between being a man or a woman took their place.

They found it easy to find the evidence for their arguments. They took a cool look at the so-called sexual division of labour, for example, and found that the different roles occupied by the male and female workforce were not related predominantly to muscle or physical size, but to social values and attitudes about men and women. This was evident even by the 1970s and became much more obvious once the silicon chip revolutionised the nature of work and made any biological differences virtually irrelevant. It is significant that gender differentials remain in most areas of work, even in those areas where work does not require hard physical labour and where women and men have been equally trained for the same task. Men still overwhelmingly occupy the most well-paid, higher-status positions and in some areas it has been a sustained battle for women to be accepted at all. The pre-modern justification was that men and women are biologically suited for different areas of work (and levels of pay!). But there is little evidence for this, especially in most of the professions or the business world. It is much more to do with how women and men are evaluated, who makes the decisions and how hierarchies are designed.

There are complex issues at stake in other areas of male-female relationships. Take, for example, the area of violence towards women. It had been long assumed under pre-modern notions that domestic violence, incest or sexual assault were caused largely by instinctual, biological urges which men could not control. Indeed, sociobiology suggested that this is an inevitable part of the way societies evolve. Yet it is now much more widely recognized that much violence towards women is the result of the deliberate excercise of male power, aided by the unconscious collusions of a male-dominant society. To relate it simply to uncontrollable primitive drives and instincts grossly misses the point. Indeed, some researchers argue that such violence is often very controlled. A general practitioner called in to treat many women subject to domestic violence documents how precise and measured such attacks can be. He points out that a domestic abuser will often assault his victim to the very point of suffocation, but relinquish hold at exactly the time needed before she is asphyxiated.[7]

It is interesting, in passing, to ask why so much violence in the home has traditionally gone unreported. This is also true in cases of rape, especially when the rapist is known to the victim. The reasons are not unrelated to the discussion. One predominant response from the victims is that they feel ashamed. (This is true incidentally, whether the violence is suffered by either women or men.) They feel that the behaviour of a violent spouse, partner or colleague reflects negatively on their own value and worth, and on their 'femininity' or 'masculinity'. It is a telling indication of the force of social attitudes. In a different context of violence, shame from the victim would not be the response. If a storekeeper, for example, were to endure a brutal assault to himself during a burglary he might feel angry and outraged, or cautious and nervous in the future. But he is unlikely to feel ashamed. Values which attach themselves to gendered behaviour are very complex and are shaped both by current ideologies of men and women, and also by power structures.

Power and Patriarchy

This concept of power is therefore one of the key socio-political hinges of the modernists. They argue that it lies at the heart of both economic relations and sexual ones (the 'Personal is also Political') and in this conjunction lies the ability to create patriarchy. Speaking bluntly, we have constructed cultures which have rewarded men for being men, and penalised women for being women. Built into most of these societies are attitudes and

---

[7] See Trevor Stammers, *When Love Lies Bleeding* (London: Hodder & Stoughton, 1996). See also James Alsdurf and Phyllis Alsdurf, *Battered into Submission* (Downers Grove: IVP, 1989); Carol J. Adam, *Women Battering* (Minneapolis: Fortress, 1994); Nancy Nason-Clark, *The Battered Wife: How Christians Confront Family Violence* (Louiseville: Westminster John Knox Press, 1997).

practices which divide men and women into different groups with clearly distinctive roles, and then reinforce and elevate men's role, whilst belittling or even deriding women's. Reality itself has been viewed predominantly through the standpoint of the male, and consequently we have not questioned the idea that men should be the dominant sex and women the subservient. The problem is that cultures have fooled millions of people into thinking this is normal. Yet there is nothing that is simply normal or natural. What becomes accepted as 'normal' in any given society is a social and political construct of those in power, by the elites who are able to maintain the *status quo*.

To illustrate their point, modernist writers offered a very different reading of our early, post-war gender history. The argument which poured vehemently out of this new consciousness insisted that 'normality' was ideologically reconstructed in the 1950s to ensure that the key task of the day could be accomplished. Far from being natural and biological it was driven by political motivation. Even during the war, gender roles had not simply gone along 'biological' lines. Although women had not been part of the fighting forces, they had contributed to the war economy in many capacities, not only in jobs of domestic service, nursing, ancillary and clerical services, but in munitions, heavy industry, and manufacturing. Women had worked as ship-builders, welders, furnace-workers, engine drivers – in fact in all the jobs previously believed to be only feasible as men's work. Even muscular work was shown to be not fundamentally about simple muscle power, but about organisation, co-operation, team spirit, where the women involved enjoyed the comradeship of production. But what happened at the end of the war was interesting. Certainly in Britain and the rest of Europe most women were only too glad to get away from the furnaces and back to the home. But not all, and in many parts of the USA the movement back was strongly resisted. In the film *Rosie the Rivetter*, a Brooklyn Jewish woman was one of those who told her story. She explained how all the long years of war, when she had been working as a first grade welder in a munitions factory, she had one dream. She wanted in peace-time to make something beautiful and creative out of the iron which was used for killing, in particular to make a magnificent, ornate wrought-iron gate. Yet her dream was never realized because she, like the others, was summarily dismissed. They were required to vacate their jobs for the returning men, and go back to housework or domestic ancilary employment. From being productive and esteemed she was now involuntarily 'unproductive', doing non-work as far as official statistics and social status were concerned.

In writings and film the post-war period was exposed not as one of 'normal' outworking of 'natural' gender roles, but as being the time when normality was reinvented to suit the ideology of the decision-makers. No government could afford to have a large unemployment situation for the returning servicemen after the war. There would soon be serious questions about the sacrifice of life if a powerful force of men trained for fighting could not be honoured by meaningful work. So women had to go. Government propaganda films were part of the process. Women who had previously worked alongside men and been encouraged to leave their children in the crèche were now rebuked for being heartless mothers. Housewives who had been given survival recipes for food for immediate consumption were now given recipes which took four days to cook. By exposing this archive material, and giving their own interpretation of what had happened, the feminists of the 1970s and beyond challenged every explanation which appealed simplistically to biology and showed its flaws.

The Captive Wife?

The pre-modern notion had been that women's family roles had also been based on their sex differences. Being by nature more nurturing, it was natural that they and not men should be in charge of raising children. Being by nature more instinctual, they should be in the home where these traits could flourish. So, even though they did not contribute to the hard economic production necessary for any society to survive, women's biology equipped them for the childrearing and domestic work which provided a supportive substructure for the work process.

New research in the social sciences began to challenge all that. To start with the premise was attacked as false. Women weren't raising children because they were hard-wired to be more loving, but because they were shut out of higher education and discriminated against in the paid labour force.[8] When this changed, and women were admitted equally to these areas the likelihood was that the ideology of woman-as-homemaker would change. Next, the idea that women were 'unproductive' in the home was attacked. Every society's economy depended on the 'unpaid' services of women.

A new interest in gender was also reflected in studies on domesticity. Areas once deemed too insignificant for study now became noteworthy. Anne Oakley wrote a substantial study on the *Sociology of Housework*, following it with a best-selling paperback, *Housewife: Low Cost, High Value*.[9] She documented widespread disatisfaction with the monotony, fragmentation and relentlessness of the work of women whose lives were spent predominantly in keeping home.[10] Their biology did not fit them for that! Hannah Gavron's book, *The Captive Wife*,[11] looked at women's perceptions of intimate relationships within the home, and again the picture was not one of unparalled bliss. The younger women in her sample compared their mothers' expectations with their own, and already there was a new picture of what was being expected in marriage: not a reinforcement of old roles, but a development of new intimacy. Women wanted husbands who would cherish them and treat them as equals and companions. (The fact that in Britain three quarters of all divorces are now initiated by women suggests, sadly, that they feel this message has not always got through.)

---

[8] Kate Fillion, *Lip Service: The Myth of Female Virtue in Love, Sex and Friendship* (London: HarperCollins, 1996) p. 11.

[9] Ann Oakley, *The Sociology of Housework* (London: Robertson, 1974); *Housewife: Low Cost, High Value* (Harmondsworth: Penguin, 1976). See also, *Becoming a Mother* (Oxford: Martin Robertson, 1979).

[10] *Housewife*, p. 100.

[11] Hannah Gavron, *The Captive Wife* (London: Routledge and Kegan Paul, 1968).

The underlying assumptions of these writers of modernity were thus at odds with their pre-modern antecendents. With the focus now on gender, not sex, there was a different response to inequality. Whereas the former had believed that inequality was a justifiable and predictable outworking of biological difference, the latter believed that it was due to the exercise of power relationships, and never justifiable. The new analysis could never remain merely analytical. Once the diagnosis had been given, it inevitably must lead to the kind of action which would bring about more equal relationships. And that required the willingness of men to give up power and to be ready for change.

Equality, Similarity, and Difference

If the underlying assumption of the pre-moderns was, therefore, biological 'difference' the focus of equality feminism was 'similarity'. ('It is virtually impossible to separate the idea of equality from the idea of similarity.')[12] It now seemed that the deep similarity between women and men had been masked by the constructions of a gender identity which was oppositional. 'Far from being an expression of natural differences exclusive gender identity is the suppression of natural similarities.'[13] Unequal treatment, unequal access to power, unequal participation in decision-making all hide those similarities, and so the task of feminism is to challenge and change these structures. Once there is a commitment to change, any differences in biology will no longer be relevant to how the lives of men and women are lived out in society.

Not all feminists were in agreement with this analysis however. Separatist feminists were not interested in working alongside men in an attempt to bridge the gap caused by a patriarchal society, for, as far as they were concerned, men

---

[12] Greer, *The Whole Woman*, p. 307.

[13] G. Rubin, 'The Traffic in Women: Notes on the "political economy" of sex' in R.R. Reitr (ed.), *Toward and Anthropology of Women* (New York: Monthly Review Press, 1975) pp. 179–180.

themselves constituted the problem. The important issue for them was straightforward: to effect a radical improvement in the lives of women. But when women had been not only marginalised, but actually defined, by assumptions of patriarchy, the first task was to challenge those definitions and to allow women to speak for themselves. So, in order for women to develop their own voice they needed space from men, and they needed space in every area where they had previously been subordinated by men. Separatist feminists criticised equality feminism as optimistic and naive. It was optimistic in its view of social change and naive in its assumptions about the effectiveness of legislation. A search for equality keeps men constantly in view, but an assertion of difference offers more openness.

However, most people recognized that whether they argued for equality or difference, this in no way guarantees liberation for women. In a society where those who have the privileges and do not want to lose them, arguments can always be 'neutralized' by clever footwork. Germaine Greer points out.

> A male soldier who wants the right to wear long hair pleads equality; a male tennis player who wants to go on being paid twice as much as his mixed doubles partner will plead difference. A man who wants paternity leave will plead equality, a member of the Marylebone Cricket Club (MCC) who wants to exclude women will plead difference.[14]

Real freedom depends more on the structures and attitudes which lie underneath the appeal to either similarity or difference and many of those are not open to logic.

A New Essentialism

Although the thrust of modernism was to be anti-essentialist, it was clear that the modernists did not dispense with essentialism altogether. They had their own explanatory frameworks, their

---

[14] Greer, *The Whole Woman*, p. 308.

own 'metanarratives'. They replaced the metanarratives of the pre-moderns – biology, natural order, normality – with new ones which more clearly fitted their own assumptions, and the focus differed depending on whether they were liberal moderns, socialist moderns or radical moderns.[15] Where they all agreed was in the identification of the problem: that biology and nature had been offered as a justification for inequality and oppression. Where they disagreed was in how they identified its source. Liberal moderns (predominantly equality feminists) argued that it was a result of poor education, no representation and unequal legislation, and thus set about reforming the education and legal systems, helping more women in positions of authority, decision-making and leadership. The socialist moderns said it was a result of a deeper problem: economic injustice and the class system. They saw a strong parallel between production and reproduction and argued that women form an underclass behind men. So they threw their weight into a critique of capitalism and a political programme for the future.

The radicals (usually separatist feminists) rejected both these ways out, deriding both the legislative and socialist utopias. In their view socialist men were just as sexist as capitalist men. In capitalism man exploits man. In socialism it is the other way round! In fact neither care about the oppression of women. So a new diagnosis of the problem was born, focusing not on representation, legislation or economic inequality, but *men*. The radicalism was typified in the organisation SCUM (the Society for Cutting Up Men). 'Patriarchy' became the key concept to describe the relations between men and women. And what did patriarchy use to justify male dominance? Biology and sexuality. Sexuality was political and had been interpreted by a deeply sexist system. The allegation was that whether in marriage and family relationships, in incest, rape or sexual violence, women's sexuality was seen as belonging to men. Heterosexuality itself was not about equal sexual relations. It was about 'men first'. For the radical moderns, men had captured 'normality', interpreted it in ways which suited them and used it against women.

---

[15] Elaine Storkey, *What's Right With Feminism* (London: SPCK, 1985). Part 2 offers an analysis of this classification.

This radical reading of feminism, especially with regard to sexuality, was to set the scene for a new series of debates. It was also to provoke some vehement reactions from those who saw it as overstating the difference between male and female behaviour.[16]

The Assessment from Within Feminism

Today's climate is complex because much of the feminism which came out of the modernist ethos is itself under attack. It is dismissed as irrelevant by the 'new woman' because women have 'now got what they want', and simultaneously rejected by postmoderns because it is impossible to make universal statements about what 'women' want. Yet, even though postmodernity has redrafted the terms of the conversation, modernism, like pre-modernity, has not disappeared in the discourse on sex and gender. For, at the turn of the century, a new generation of young feminists is writing from within the modernist metanarrative.

Some of the arguments published, rehearsed in Natasha Walter's book *The New Feminism*, for example, sound suprisingly like the old liberal feminism of the 1960s.[17] In *On the Move*, published in 1999, a group of young women writers go over the same concerns that affected their 'modernist' mothers and grandmothers, with very similar arguments and conclusions. Katherine Viner and Aminatta Forna believe women have been taken in by the lure of the pay packet and the sense of equality in the workplace. They look at the way top women executives are being persuaded to pose in girlie positions for men's magazines, and challenge the notion that this is about liberation. Viner argues that at the end of the century the personal is more political than ever: 'more political than when gender roles were more stratified because there is more up for grabs.' Even if it had been achieved, equality at

---

[16] Fillion, *Lip Service*, pp. 198–261.
[17] Natasha Walter, *The New Feminism* (London: Little Brown, 1998). See also my review 'The Same Old Story?' in *Third Way* (Harrow, Middx) Vol. 21, No. 6, July/Aug 1998, pp. 12–14, and 'Still Moving' in *Third Way*, Vol. 21, No. 4, May 1999.

work would not be enough. For women's *sexuality* is still
defined by a patriarchal society. For Viner, accepting the
principle of equal pay means little if women do not have 'the
right for their body size to be unimportant, or . . . the right to
an equal sexual relationship.'[18]

This is echoed by a reassessment of the gains by someone
who has been in the forefront of feminism over the last thirty
years. In *The Whole Woman* Germaine Greer notes that in
many areas of women's lives the situation for them is worse
than it was when she wrote *The Female Eunuch*. She questions whether even the changes in the law delivered for
women the freedom that they were intended to. For when the
power of patriarchy itself does not diminish, every piece of
legislation can eventually become another way of producing
oppression for women. In a poignant passage she wonders
what ultimately women won even with the reform of the
abortion law:

> What women 'won' was the 'right' to undergo invasive proce-
> dures in order to terminate unwanted pregnancies, unwanted
> not just by them but by their parents, their sexual partners, the
> governments who would not support mothers, the employers
> who would not employ mothers, the landlords who would not
> accept tenants with children, the schools that would not accept
> students with children. What abortion did was to make illiberal
> governments seem feminist.[19]

It is interesting that apart from these latest books the debate
had been taking a new direction. A new genre had begun to
shape and represent the questions about sex and gender. The
postmodern response had already bitten deeply into the
feminism of the 1960s and 1970s and challenged its own
assumptions. But it was not simply some despondency with
the *results* of the feminism of modernity which triggered off

---

[18] Katherine Viner, 'The Personal is Still Political' in Natasha Walter
(ed.) *On the Move: Feminism For a New Generation* (London:
Virago, 1999) p. 24.
[19] Greer, *The Whole Woman*, p. 86.

the postmodern response. It was a shift of philosophical underpinnings. The question whether our sexuality is constructed or created was to be taken to a new emphasis. Modernity based its arguments on a distinction between sex (created) and gender (constructed). Postmodernity began to reject the differentiation between sex and gender and argue instead that all identity, indeed sexuality itself, was constructed. As Hubbard had said in 1981, 'in our critique of biology, one thing becomes clear, not only must we not believe that biology is our destiny, we must re-examine whether it is even our biology.'[20]

Women also began to contest the concept of equality, identifying the paradox which, as Elaine Graham points out, lies at the heart of feminist political claims. '(I)n asserting equality with men, feminists refer to shared experiences of oppression, which are identified as unique and distinctive to women alone.'[21] This uniqueness which now became the focus and thinking was once again predicated on difference – although a different difference from that of pre-modernity. Gone was the essentialism of biology, but gone also was the essentialism of modernity: the location of gender identity in patterns of learning, expectations and power structures. For postmodernity, there are no essentials, no metanarratives, no overriding explanatory frameworks. Even the ubiquitous notion of the patriarchal oppression of women has to be understood as itself a construction. What was to follow was to shake the contours of the debate and take it into another new phase.

---

[20] R. Hubbard, 'The Emperor Doesn't Wear Any Clothes: The Impact of Feminism on Biology' in Dale Spender (ed.), *Men's Studies Modified* (Oxford: Pergamon, 1981) p. 217.

[21] Graham, *Making the Difference*, p. 170.

Chapter Four

The Postmodern Experience

Notwithstanding the sudden revival at the end of the twentieth century, the arguments of modernity had increasingly receded over the last decade. Eight years before, French postmodern writer, Luce Irigaray, insisted that we are now 'at a different stage of History.'[1] Five years ago Jean Joseph Goux suggested that the modernist phase may be coming to a close. Its concerns had been superceded, its battles were not now relevant. For Goux, the cultural changes had finally seen off the old ways of thinking. In particular, the obsession with defeating the biological essentialists had run its course. 'One might go so far as to say: essentialism is no longer a danger for it is no longer even thinkable. . . . In a world dominated by the market and the media . . . and the inconvertibility of circulating values, something completely different is at stake.'[2]

For postmodern people, that 'something different' is the ability to live with the fluidity of shifting images and styles. It is the capacity to negotiate our own identity without needing someone else to define for us who we are. For in a market-media reality we recognize there are a multiplicity of options from which to shape our own style and choose our own values. We do not need to battle against outmoded world-views or absolutist explanations in order to try to establish an 'Archimedean' point, for there can be no such vantage point

---

[1] Luce Irigaray, *J'aime à toi: Esquisse d'une félicité dans l'histoire* (Paris: Grasset, 1992) p. 72.
[2] J.J. Goux, 'Irigaray vs the Utopia of the Neutral Sex' in C. Burke et al., *Engaging with Irigaray*, p. 180.

outside the constructs which fashion who we are, from which we can survey reality. We need simply to learn to live at ease within a pluralism of meanings and choices.

For most social commentators postmodernity marks the end of any single, unifying world-view which attempts to offer universally valid explanations. It makes little difference to the postmodern mind whether those explanations were based on concepts of biology or power structures. They were still making an appeal to some grand narrative, some fundamental set of values or explanatory framework which would hold good for all times. Such an endeavour is now seen as fundamentally mistaken. As D. Harvey explains in his study, postmodernity represents a 'total acceptance of the ephemeral fragmentation and discontinuity of life'.[3] Postmodern concerns are with surface rather than depth, with representations rather than the search for ultimate truth. For what is truth? Only what Nietzsche suggested: 'a mobile army of metaphors, metonyms and anthropomorphisms'.[4] So we do not need to draw any demarcation between representation and reality, for images are as 'real' as anything which purports to lie behind them. And we do not need to study the past to try to find 'truth' there, for the past is significant only in its ability to be experienced in the present. In postmodern culture, present experience is the only reality we know, and we can know it without trying to grasp any extra dimension of 'meaning' outside the process of experience. For language, image and experience come together, playfully and creatively, their meaning constructed or decided according to cultural convention. We are part of the constructive process, presenting them as pastiche, metaphors, symbol, styles or options which we may accept or reject as we wish.

A postmodern critique is therefore as much of the modernists as of the pre-modernists, for neither have escaped intransigence. Its own commitment is to deconstruction, the questioning and dismantling of all that we previously thought was real. There are no boundaries to what can be deconstructed: it includes the past, the present, categorical explanations,

---

[3] D. Harvey, *The Condition of Postmodernity*, Oxford, Blackwell 1989 p.44.

[4] Friedrich Nietzche, *Notebooks* (1873).

concepts, language, meaning, sexuality, biology, sociology and theology. In the process of deconstruction we discover that the 'absolutes' of the past are only particulars, and even these particulars can be seen through a myriad different perspectives depending on the location of the perceiver. Lars Johansson sums up the procedure and its effects:

> The postmodern deconstructs the metanarrative of the Western tradition, leaving us with a plurality of narratives and values. One of the metanarratives that has been disclosed is reason. Central to the critique of reason is language. All thinking begins and ends in language. Philosophy is seen as rhetoric in disguise. There is no independent vantage point outside language.[5]

The result is a position which locates us always within some discourse, whose parameters are structured by the words and concepts which give it meaning. There is no shared meta-language reflecting a reality which exists outside particular discourses. What is more, the words we use, the *signifiers*, do not signify that something actually does exist 'outside' the words, for 'signification only ever refers back to itself, that is to say to another signification. Each time we are obliged in the analysis of language to look for the signification of a word, the only correct method is to enumerate all of its uses.'[6] It is simply the use of language which decides its meaning, not any correspondence to some reality which exists outside.

This view has had repercussions in many disciplines, not simply in cultural or linguistic studies. It has been one of the prevailing influences in contemporary theology, not least in the earlier views of Don Cupitt, often referred to as the 'Sea of Faith'. It has been expressed as an 'outsidelessness' position, the view 'that there is nothing beyond or outside human beings, neither God nor some other notion like "Ultimate

---

[5] Lars Johansson, 'New Age – A Synthesis of the Pre-modern, Modern and Postmodern' in P. Sampson, V. Samuel and C. Sugden (eds.), *Faith and Modernity* (Oxford: Regnum, 1984) p. 216.

[6] Jacques-Alain Miller (ed.), *The Seminar of Jacques Lacan, Book 1* (trans. John Forrester; Cambridge: Cambridge University Press, 1988) p. 238.

Reality" that gives life and meaning and purpose."[7] Language is 'a disastrous mental illusion' from which there is no escape.

If language constructs reality, we can bring anything into being. Our words create politics, sexuality, history, God. In that sense the *word* is more powerful than it has ever been. But it has an uncertain and ambiguous power: not the power of 'rendering past lives more coherent and less conflictful than they were' but the power to 'recognize the instability of all categories, the contested terrain of all historical sites, the dangers in all political projects.'[8] For what is left of history, other than competing interpretations of the present? What is sexuality other than ideas in the mind? And who is God, other than a concept shaped by those who wish to give a name to an experience?

Deconstructing Modernist Feminism

In this climate, the language of modernity is seen to have had deep internal contradictions, especially within the discourse of equality feminism. As Elaine Graham explains:

> Deconstructionist philosophies and strategies claim that 'equality' and 'difference' are not absolutes, but are themselves constructs. They emerge from human discourse and exist within a context of power relations and material practice. To attempt to impose absolute and unchanging meaning on gender relations is to assert an abstraction which returns us to metaphysics.[9]

However, within modernity, language about sex and gender was still being used as though there was some fixed meaning to these terms: something that post existed objectively. The modernists believed they had highlighted the part that social construction plays in our identity. They thought they had eliminated

---

[7] David A. Hart, *Faith in Doubt: Non-Realism and Christian Belief* (London: Mowbray, 1993) p. 7.

[8] N.A. Hewitt, 'Compounding Differences' in *Feminist Studies* 18.2 (1992) p. 317.

[9] Graham, *Making the Difference*, p. 185.

essentialism by changing the categories from sex to gender. Some of them conceded that our sexuality might in some sense be biologically 'given', but did not see that as important, for even if sexual differences do exist objectively, they are of limited significance and always subsumed under the dynamic of gender. Yet they failed to recognize that the attempt to avoid biological determinism by emphasizing a sex/gender distinction simply opened up a different form of absolutism. Cultural roles, patterns of learning and socially imposed norms became, rather than biology, the new constituents of gender identity. There was always some reference to an objective reality 'out there', an explanatory framework which gave our signfiers meaning. However far it had moved, then, from the notion of creation to construction, modernity was still working with the notion of a 'core identity' to ourselves and our relationships.

There were other problems too. Modernity had attempted to critique and replace the system of male domination with a radical egalitarianism. For postmodern writers, it was inevitable that this challenge would ultimately fail because equality feminism never escaped the assumptions of the system it tried to undermine. As far as Goux is concerned it did not see that its own language and concepts absorbed the very male domination it was trying to counter, for, 'without intending it, egalitarian claims are complicit with the deep logic of this domination.'[10] Equality feminism rests too heavily on the notion of similarity, and underplays the significance of sex in favour of gender. It fails to recognize that 'both "sex" and "gender" are woven of multiple, asymmetrical strands of difference, charged with multifaceted, dramatic narratives of domination and struggle.'[11] Indeed, the postmoderns allege, within the modernist critique sex disappears altogether as a significant category. Everything is swallowed up by gender. But by which gender? Irigaray and others are quite clear: the

---

[10] Goux, 'Irigaray', p. 180.

[11] D. Haraway, 'Investment Strategies for the Evolving Portfolio of Primate Females' in M. Jacobus, E. Fox Keller and S. Shuttleworth (eds.), *Body/Politics: Women and the Discourses of Science* (London: Routledge, 1990) p. 140.

male gender. The norm remains male. Equality is predicated on women's parity *with men*.

The assumption had been that to lift gender roles out of power relationships would bring both equality and gender neutrality. Yet, for those who take a postmodern stance, it could never do this. An egalitarianism which rests on the abandonment of difference is the most subtle way yet of making women invisible. For tradition, language and concepts have all, for too long, been formed within a male-dominant framework. Espousing 'equality', whilst everything else stays the same is to give the appearance of power to women, whilst denying the reality of it. It is in fact to capitulate to the deeper structures of patriarchy in the name of reform. Egalitarianism in effect means the disappearance of women. They are admitted into the structures as token or lesser men. According to Irigaray, for a woman to abandon her own sexual identity 'represents the greatest possible submission to masculine culture.'[12] Women simply become absorbed within the male gender, what Irigaray calls the 'masculine-neutral'.

Where does that leave women's authenticity? Trapped in something 'suicidal', 'the worst expression of the extravagance of masculine intellectualism.'[13] The argument was that women's identity can never be fully realized under a gender analysis, any more than it could be realized under biological essentialism. Gender identity 'is ultimately a symptom of parasitic invasion, the expression within me of forces originating from the outside.'[14] What we must do is find who we are from *within*. It is only in the real stuff of women's sexual experience that we encounter our identity, and we must reclaim our sexuality for ourselves. Each woman has to discover her own subjectivity, stripped away from all the years of patriarchal interpretation, and she must do it as herself, in her own particularity, not as some inaccessible universal

---

[12] Luce Irigaray, *Sexes et Genres à travers les langues: élements de communication sexueé* (Paris: Grasset, 1990) p. 13.

[13] Goux, 'Irigaray', p. 182.

[14] J. Halberstam and I. Livingston, *Posthuman Bodies* (Indiana: Indiana University Press, 1995) p. viii.

'woman'. In Irigaray's words: 'Beneath all those/her appear-
ances, beneath all those/her borrowed finery, that female
other still sub-sits.'[15] So sex becomes deconstructable and
reconstructable into experiences which women can choose to
appropriate for themselves.

Created or Constructed?

We thus arrive at the furthest point from the notion that our
sexuality and human identity have some kind of fixed, irreduc-
ible centre, and it is precisely here that the postmodern writers
return to the concept of difference. They are no longer afraid
of the essentialism, the notions of fixed sexual identity which
had kept women locked into submission, for, as Goux
believes, it is now out of view. They recognize the suspicion
and misunderstandings which might greet this move back to a
concept which has a chequered history, 'and the guarantees it
will need to offer if it is not simply to be confused with a return
to pre-modern prejudices'.[16] But this sexual difference is no
longer predicated on anything that is 'natural' or fixed or
defined within a masculine-shaped reality. Difference is now
self-defined and fluid. As Moi points out: 'Differences always
take us elsewhere, we might say, involve us in an ever prolifer-
ating network of displacement and deferral of meaning.'[17]

At one level, therefore, postmodernity offers a far more
intense critique of gender than anything that has come before.
For it challenges the very linguistic processes we use as being
imbued with masculine-constructed meaning. What the
modernist writers had offered as processes of differentiating,
separating, analysing are now seen themselves as gender-
loaded. For all of these are activities shaped within a discourse
dominated by the masculine. Even the terms of the debate to

---

[15] Luce Irigaray, *Marine Lover of Friedrich Nietszche* (trans. Gillian
C. Gill; New York: Columbia University Press, 1991) p. 118.
[16] Goux, 'Irigaray', p. 188.
[17] Toril Moi, *Sexual/Textual Politics* (London: Routledge, 1988)
p. 154.

which this book is committed are questionable. We have been talking as though 'constructed' or 'created' refer to two polar opposites, two competing explanations, which we decide upon by reference to arguments which match the realities and facts 'out there'. But for postmodernity these are precisely the thought forms which have predominated in a male-shaped discourse. What is more, there is no 'out there', and these are themselves only linguistic constructs.

The only viable way forward in opening up an understanding of identity and sexuality has to be through experience. For Irigaray and Kristeva this means through women's experience. For an increasing number of male writers it means through men's experience. But this process cannot be regarded as reaching out towards any new kind of essentialism for just as women and men are different, and men and men are different, so women are different from each other. We have to reject some uniform notion of human experience or even of sexual-gendered experience, and see that 'difference itself is multiple, conditioned by the factors of class, region, sexuality and culture'.[18] With a focus on narrative rather than analysis we listen to and absorb the experiences of all women: black and white, rich and poor, powerful and marginalised, immigrant and indigenous, straight and gay, old and young. It is not the job of the theorist to choose between them or to pass any judgement on them. We simply hear their stories.

So, just as there can be no one gender analysis of the oppression of women, so there is no one sexual analysis of the identity of women. Our sexuality, like all the rest of life, is in the constant process of construction. The problem will be in moving from critique to action, from deconstruction to a new ethical imperative. For nothing is being offered as the way forward. Nothing is held up for us to appropriate. Neither natural sexuality nor gender equality shapes any new engagement. What we have instead is 'the quest for a social and cultural sexuation whose eventual outcome one cannot, by definition, foresee, any more than one can

---

[18] Graham, *Making the Difference*, p. 173.

invent overnight the characteristic forms and style of a civilization'.[19]

So, Who am I?

All of this has predictable consequences. The first point is that we have to make our own way; decide for ourselves what it is to be a woman or a man. Philip and Miriam Sampson make the obvious point:

> Once our 'natural sexuality' ceases to define a 'real woman' (or man) it is obvious that there is no 'natural' way of being a 'man' at all for there are a wide variety of cultural styles of masculinity to choose from or to combine: from Rambo to Julian Clary, from the 'new laddism' to the 'new man', from straight to gay. Gender identity is constructed, not inherited, and is composed of an amalgam of images which already exist in the culture around us.[20]

But this puts enormous emphasis on the process of choosing an identity, especially where there are no constraints on choice. But how do we choose when there are no underlying ethical reasons why some choices are good and others are bad? Having the freedom and space to choose from a multiplicity of identities is not much gain if it does not matter what I choose. There can be no coherent critique of those who choose to reinforce old patriarchal lifestyles, if this, after all, is their preference. The muddy waters of relativism are never far from a postmodern critique. And relativism can never give us a framework for strategies for change.

But it is not only that difference is 'unable to reflect the complexity of lived experience at the same time as sketching a theoretical reconfiguration.'[21] Nor is it that only choice

---

[19] Goux, 'Irigaray', p. 189.

[20] Philip and Miriam Sampson, 'Looking the Parts', *Third Way*, Vol. 20, No. 8, Oct 1997, p. 22.

[21] Graham, *Making the Difference*, p. 173.

becomes thereby emptied as a concept With postmodern fragmentation begins the erasure of the category of self. We move from being who and what we are as the result of some personal essence, to how we are constructed in various social groups, where 'the initial stages of this consciousness result in a sense of the self as a social con artist, manipulating images to achieve ends'. But who or what is it that is being constructed? For even to talk of the construction of self implies something I can identify as personal identity. 'As the category of "real self" continues to recede from view, however, one acquires a pastiche-like personality.'[22]

The other unanswered question is whether postmodernity can ever deliver a version of difference which avoids all the essentialist pitfalls derided by its pre-modern and modern predecessors. For how can we locate or even talk about women's difference unless we describe it in terms that are identifiable? And once we have identified it, whether in terms of the 'jouissance' of some pre-oedipal stage[23] or the existence of some 'feminine fluidity – inner space, movement, flux, becoming', why is this not also a kind of essentialism? The answer is not clear, except insofar as deconstructionists assert that they are simply creating limited analogies and not developing a theory of being. Irigaray believes that in discovering and constructing their own sexuality, women are not unearthing anything which exists independently, uncontaminated by patriarchal values. Authentic sexuality is rather the development of 'sites of resistance' to such values. Similarly, in offering us a concept of 'polymorphous sensuality', Irigaray insists she is not offering this as 'a 'true' or accurate description of women. Its function is not referential, but combative: '. . . It does not designate a female essence or anatomy but subverts the dominant male conceptions of women's essence.'[24] But this is dangerously close to semantics and

[22] K.J. Gergen, *The Saturated Self*, (London, Basic Books 1990) p. 170.
[23] L. Irigaray, *Speculum of the Other Woman* (trans. Gillian C. Gill; Ithaca: Cornell University Press, 1985) pp. 140–4.
[24] Elizabeth A. Grosz, *Sexual Subversions: Three French Feminists* (Sydney: Allen and Unwin, 1989) p. 116.

rhetoric. It seems to be saying little more than that a description of what constitutes female difference is not really a description. It is simply a denial of a patriarchal construction and as such leaves everything open. It is at this cost that postmodernity retains both plurality and fragmentation, and nudges women into designing their own subjectivity.

With the postmodern response our journey thus arrives at a place of ambiguity and uncertainty. At best, we might describe postmodern writings as playing, ironically, with old patriarchal concepts of sexuality, using them to shape an alternative position. More realistically we might feel that we are trapped within a self-referencing system. For when words are used without any suggestion that any the models to which they refer actually exist, then the meaning of language becomes fraught with complications. What is more, how do we know when to stop deconstructing and accept the position we have now arrived at? Nothing within the deconstruction process can help us with that. Instead, we are caught up in an infinite regress, where each deconstruction can be further deconstructed, and no single text can ever make a definitive statement.[25] In this way we *cannot say* whether human sexual identity is constructed and not created, for each of these terms are themselves linguistic constructions, signifying nothing beyond. We cannot even say what constitutes gender identity for, ultimately, there is no identity to be had, only a series of experiences.

The question is, then, where do we go from here? And the answer is not clear. But as we shall see later, the lack of clarity has not prevented a postmodern perspective from finding its way into some areas of feminist theology. There, as everywhere, it throws up challenges for others which, from its own perspective, it cannot meet itself.

---

[25] See Carolyn Burke's essay 'Irigaray Through the Looking Glass' in C. Burke et al., *Engaging with Irigaray*, pp. 37–56.

Chapter Five

Gender and 'Difference' in Popular Writings

Unlike the modernist feminism of the 1960s, the writings of the postmodern theorists have not translated readily from academia to a good fireside read. Admittedly, the academic sophistication of Luce Irigaray, Jean Joseph Goux or Rosi Brandotti was not evident in such 1960s popular blockbusters as Betty Friedan's *The Second Sex* or Germaine Greer's *Female Eunuch*. Yet these were important books which both reflected and influenced the scholarship current at the time. The uncompromising critique and polemic analysis of the social science writings were also there in the popular bestsellers. Readers did not flinch from the calls for a dismantling of power structures, but rather took the volumes cheerfully to bed with them. The attraction of these books was that they were accessible to anyone interested in society or gender. Not everyone may have agreed with what they read, but they could certainly understand it. By contrast, postmodern feminist theorists seem quite out of reach for most of the contemporary reading public. They do not suggest themselves as pleasant after-dinner relaxation or travel easily as comfortable holiday reading. In fact, they seem to frighten off anyone who does not enjoy probing philosophical concepts, or a complex francophone style of writing.

Paradoxically, postmodern feminist theorists are also alleged to be out of touch with the women's movement. In fact from the early days of Irigaray's writings (she had previously been regarded as a 'lesbian separatist'), those who still represented that movement were quick to hit back at her, accusing her of misrepresenting them. They disliked the implication that postmodernity had 'seen through' their own 'limitations'. They rebuffed the accusation that their own arguments had been narrow, focusing on a single cause of oppression. This was not the case, they insisted, for '(t)he explosion of writing, the multiplication of references were used in quite the opposite way, to suggest the diversity of outside influences and states of freedom conquered or rediscovered. Jubilation in all directions over new ways of life!' This breadth for them had now disappeared and so had the radical vision: 'Luce Irigaray, by contrast, brings the most reactionary possible feelings into her work . . . How could this changeless body be the source of a new destiny?'[1]

It is not only the self-congratulation of the postmodern writers which has got up their critics' noses. It is also their alleged obscurantism and self-indulgence. What is the point of lengthy analyses of women's 'subjective inner space' when women's 'public external space' is still vulnerable to violence, rape and attack? Why waste precious time with erudite articles on 'sites of jouissance' when so many women are still struggling with sites of poverty, single parenthood or inadequate health resources? The irritation is evident. It is as if these new theorists never intended their writings to be read by 'ordinary' readers with ordinary concerns. They seemed instead to write either simply for themselves or for a few, other, elitist scholars.

When the key contemporary theorists are inaccessible to a mass readership it is interesting to reflect on what has filled the gap between the scholars and the populace. There are certainly contemporary best-sellers on male-female issues. And they certainly involve themselves with current key problems. But those that have been sending their authors laughing to the bank since the mid-1990s are very unlike the 1960s' and 1970s' tirades against power structures or the politics of gender.[2] What

---

[1] Christine Fauré, 'The Twilight of the Goddesses, or The Intellectual Crisis of French Feminism' (trans. Lillian S. Robinson) *Signs: Journal of Women in Culture and Society*, Vol. 7, No. 11 (1981) p. 81.

[2] This has changed with the response to Walter (ed.), *On the Move*, and Greer, *The Whole Woman*.

has replaced these on the shelves of railway bookshops have been predominantly books of popular gender psychology. Many are light-hearted, some are polemic, some are tedious. But, significantly, almost all of them focus on the idea of *difference*. They have reflected the newly revived interest in difference without the academic focus or background.

The very starting point for most of these authors is that women and men are different, and, for the most part, the aim seems to be to identify the points of difference and offer advice to deal with it. Unlike the popular writers of the 1960s, however, most of the currently popular authors manage with barely any reference to the theoretical debates. Few seem concerned enough to look at the philosophical underpinnings of 'difference' or to try to distinguish one theoretical viewpoint from another. There is virtually no awareness either of the discussions around essentialism. Inevitably this deficiency can have great drawbacks. Although some of these books are written by people who are aware of the complexity of gender ideas, many are not and the debate between 'nature' and 'culture' becomes confused and bowdlerised. Some writers are also stuck in belligerently pre-modern essentialist assumptions without being remotely critical of their own position.

Popular Publications – A Confused Debate

We can see this in *Why Men Don't Iron*, an archetypal book from a 'pre-modern' perspective which claims in its subtitle to be *The Real Science of Gender Studies*. It is peppered with appeals to biology and believes that all gender differences are sex differences laid down in nature. Gender cultural terms ('masculinity') are used interchangeably with sex biological terms ('maleness') with predictable results. The argument is that if we ran society along 'natural' lines, men (and thereby women) would be much happier. But men are apparently now under attack from a current political ideology which claims that they need to change, and which does not realize that 'nature' cannot be changed. So who is to blame for this new thinking? Apparently the chief culprit is postmodernity.

The authors manage to lay much of the blame at the feet of postmodernists whilst showing an embarrassing lack of understanding of the postmodern position. At times they even assume that the postmoderns are trying to *avoid* difference: 'The postmodernists want men to change, to become indeed, more like women.'[3] At the same time, the authors confidently maintain that all their own assertions about differences are backed up by something they call 'science'. 'Science has upset the egalitarian applecart by conclusively showing that the sexes are distinct in how they act and think.'[4] Yet in spite of their fascination for quasi-scientific jargon, their 'science' sounds alarmingly like tired stereotypes used for years to justify old gender roles. A few examples will make the point:

> A man enjoys a neurological high when he is faced by competition . . . a woman is not equipped by biology to receive this neurological reward. Indeed, if anything, her reaction to competition will be anxiety. (p. 192)

> His lower serotonin level also makes it difficult for him to persevere with a boring chore, because his reward circuitry is not switched on by this sort of tedious activity. (p. 255)

> The fact that men have lower monoamine oxidase levels than women means that they will be much better adapted to the pressures of high-risk jobs, whether that job is trading derivatives or landing high-performance fighters on to aircraft carriers. . . . (I)t will be a very rare woman who posseses the low serotonin needed for her brain not to engage her caution-inducing frontal cortex as she hurtles in towards the deck. (p. 159)

> Men have a lower sensitivity to detail, which means he simply does not notice the dust as she does . . . the stale socks and sweaty shirt don't bother him because they are among the pheromone-related

---

[3] Anne and Bill Moir, *Why Men Don't Iron* p. 21.
[4] ibid. p. 13.

smells that women are acutely aware of but men do not detect.
(p. 252)

Some high t(estosterone) level males do marry, but they are 43%
more likely to be divorced and 38% more likely to engage in
extramarital sex . . .The conclusion seems obvious. You can have
a man, but you cannot have a man who feels, touches, cares and
empathizes like a woman, not if you want him to stay a man.
(p. 265)

Reading books like this make us realize two things. First, that
quoting science or statistics is utterly unhelpful without the
careful research and safeguards necessary for their interpretation. Second, that Jean Joseph Goux was wrong: essentialism
is not dead. Scholars might have given it a decent burial, but
non-scholars are still capable of digging it up, dressing it in the
newest fashion, and parading it down the catwalk.

What is interesting is that in attacking the idea of gender
neutrality as a myth, these authors are oblivious of the fact
that postmodern scholars, like Goux, have got there before
them. Their reasons for the attack are, however, fundamentally different. We saw that postmodernity argues that the
gender-neutral hides a masculine bias where 'equal' women
are still subsumed under categories which reflect male values.
The new essentialists say that the gender-neutral hides a
feminine bias, where women make unreasonable demands on
men, thereby emasculating them.[5] And whilst the solution for
these new pre-moderns is also to abandon the search for
equality, it is not so that women can know the liberation of
self-assigned difference. It is rather to recreate a society which
is excited about competition, reinforces pre-modern gender
demarcations and allows men to be 'real' men.

Most other popular authors, whilst also starting from the
idea that men and women are different, do manage to avoid
the worst excesses illustrated here. Whereas *Why men don't
Iron* is lamentable in its generalisation and biological
reductionism, John Gray's book *Men are From Mars, Women*

---

[5] ibid. p. 147.

are from Venus[6] is less judgemental and somewhat more friendly. It offers itself as a 'practical guide for improving communication and getting what you want in your relationships'. It still has definite essentialist overtones ('men are like this . . . women are like this . . .') and is written from a less than self-critical male perspective, yet the aim is less to justify stereotypes than to enable people to relate better to one another. To that end it encourages women and men to identify their own needs and recognize those of the other. It is assumed of course that all men have generalised psychological needs, attitudes and understanding, which women are not likely to recognize. And, once again, these needs are natural, evolved or created, not constructed:

> Men are like rubber bands. When they pull away, they can stretch only so far before they come springing back . . . Most women are surprised to realize that even when a man loves a woman, periodically he needs to pull away before he can get closer. Men instinctively feel this urge to pull away. It is not a decision or choice. It just happens. It is neither his fault nor her fault. It is a natural cycle. (p. 92)

But Gray does not relate this 'nature' to levels of serotonin, monoamine oxidase, or needs for neurological highs. He talks of it in terms of coming from different places. Women and men live metaphorically on different planets, Venus and Mars. They are formed by different cultures, and need to learn one another's language and thought patterns. The planetary differences between them extend to every aspect of male-female relationships, including the way emotions are handled:

> When a Venusian is upset she not only uses generalities and so forth, but also is asking for a particular kind of support. She doesn't directly ask for that support because on Venus everyone knew that dramatic language implied a particular request. (p. 62)

---

[6] John Gray, *Men are From Mars, Women are From Venus* (New York: HarperCollins, 1994).

It's easy for a woman to give what she needs and forget that her favourite Martian may need something else. Likewise, men tend to focus on their needs, losing track of the fact that the kind of love they need is not always appropriate for or supportive of their favourite Venusian. (p. 134)

Martians give when they are asked. Martians pride themselves in being self-sufficient. They don't ask for help unless they really need it. On Mars it is rude to offer help unless you are first asked.
   Quite the opposite, Venusians don't wait to offer their support. When they love someone they give in any way they can. (p. 193)

Although Gray gets too carried away with his metaphor, and his book becomes repetitive and tiresome, its aim is benign. It is to release women and men from the misunderstandings and wrong expectations they have about each other. Men need to understand that women do not read their responses in the way that men would; women need to know that men do not hear what is being implied in the way women would. In that sense it takes the theme of difference, absorbs both a 'natural' and a 'cultural' perspective and then plays it through in popular psychology, wrapping it up in counselling advice. Because it claims to be even-handed in its approach and to give insights with which people can easily identify, it has become one of the most widely read texts on gender of the 1990s. Yet it rests on essentialist assumptions which are never examined.
   His later book, *Mars and Venus in the Bedroom*, is sadly far less even-handed. It regurgitates a large number of stereotypes, and works through a haggard, old agenda, especially about sexual relations. For example, Gray warns women of the danger of giving out 'rejecting messages' to their partners. Instead of refusing sexual intercourse when she doesn't feel like it, a woman should simply encourage a few 'guilt-free quickies' or offer to give him 'a hand job', otherwise the man 'may begin desiring other women who have not yet rejected him, or he may just lose interest'. Women, however, should be careful about initiating sex themselves, and especially too directly as this puts undue pressure on men to perform and they feel controlled. A woman should rather drop indirect

hints that she is in a 'hot, lusty and intense' mood by wearing 'black lace or garters', or that she wants 'sensitive, gentle and loving sex' by putting on her nightie of white silky satin. A short and loose nightgown with no panties can be worn to indicate that she is not too bothered about foreplay. Black bra and panties means she wants to be 'up on top'.[7] When Kate Fillion describes all this as 'preposterous'[8] she is not alone.

Our next author, although a much better writer, also slides between nature and culture in a way similar to Gray. At times his assumptions are that men and women are naturally different; at other times he assumes their differences are due to 'gender culture'. But this author is not writing from a quasi-counselling perspective, and his intentions are not to reinforce patriarchal stereotypes. He is novelist, humourist and essayist. Garisson Keillor's amusing and witty volume, *The Book of Guys*, absorbs both these contradictory viewpoints simultaneously, moving from one to the other depending on which better fits his illustration. So when he discusses male sexuality he comes very close to socio-biology. He writes with his typical humour, 'A monogamous man is like a bear on a bicycle. You can train him how to ride it. But he would rather be in the woods doing what all the other bears are doing.'[9] His implication here is clear (although it is obviously tongue-in-cheek, and one never knows when to take Keillor seriously): male sexuality is shaped by instincts and biological 'needs' so that monogamy is 'unnatural'. Yet, on another page he locates the differences betwen men and women not as the product of 'nature' or essential sexual characteristics but as the product of gender culture. We are what we are because of the way gender attitudes and ideas have been communicated through our upbringing and expectations. His observations are delicious:

> Girls have it better from the beginning – don't kid yourself. They were allowed to play in the house where the books were and the adults and boys were sent outside like livestock – boys were noisy

---

7 John Gray, *Mars and Venus in the Bedroom: A Guide to Lasting Romance and Passion* (New York: HarperCollins, 1995) p. 179.
8 Fillion, *Lip Service* p. 289.
9 Garrison Keillor, *The Book of Guys* (London: Faber, 1993).

and rough and girls were nice so they got to stay and we had to go. Boys ran around in the yard with toy guns going 'shwsh, shwsh' fighting wars for made up reasons and arguing about who was dead, whilst the girls stayed inside and played with dolls creating complex family groups and learning to solve problems through negotiation and role play. Which gender is better equipped to live an adult life would you guess? Is there any doubt about this? Is it even close?'[10]

In his inimitable way Keillor is here expressing what many feminist writers have also expressed: that wide-reaching gender differences have their location in the cultural demarcations that were drawn between men and women in childhood. It is this, rather than biology, which affects how they now relate to each other in adulthood. It is culture too which changes these attitudes over time and makes certain gender styles more acceptable. The problem comes when the culture of our upbringing collides with the culture of the day, when men are now required to be able to 'bake a cherry pie, make melon balls and whip up a great soufflé'.

Keillor can get away with whatever theoretical inconsistencies he holds because he is not writing as a theorist but as an entertainer and storyteller. In a popular and entertaining genre he taps into some of the issues and ideas which have been bothering academics for several decades, and yet which few academics can now make accessible. But he can also succeed in spite of inconsistencies because he brings the very ambiguities alive in his writing, and that is where his readers are. For even in our social conventions most people are not clear whether men and women are created or constructed, and most people are unsure what they want men and women to be like. So Keillor engages all our sympathies when he describes the dual messages which women and men receive from each other. The new 'acceptable' man is the one who can 'converse easily about intimate matters, participate in recreational weeping, laugh, hug, be vulnerable. But next day go into work, place the bales into the barge and tote it.'

---

[10] ibid.

The popularising of the concept of difference has thus travelled far. It can be found in books on the psychology of gender, counselling manuels, popular educational handbooks, communication surveys, socio-linguistics, and in contemporary film and television. British television sit-coms like *Men Behaving Badly* explore what happens to a contemporary laddish culture when it operates in close proximity with women. The American show *Frasier* imagines what male-female relationships are like when orchestrated by a sensitised male psychologist. Gender difference is also the bread and butter of cartoonists. Even an artist as skilful as Gary Larsen of *Far Side* draws on male fear of difference, with hilarious results. Advertisers play on male-female caricatures, sometimes upturning them for effect.

Yet some might feel that we have heard all this before. So much of the way the concept of difference is handled in the popular culture is not too dissimilar from the way it was handled in pre-modern days. Surely, comedians in music halls and men's drinking clubs have been earning good money trading on sexual differences and mother-in-law jokes for years. So what has changed? One thing is that women have entered the show. Women are articulating their own reading of these differences and, whether as theorists, essayists, dramatists or comedians are making their voices heard. It is women too who have made the more scholarly contributions, where the issues are not from the perspective of the male as norm. This decision of women to speak for themselves has changed the struture of the debate, and reflected it back from a different perspective.

Problems in Studying the Area

When we move away from simplistic generalisations, however, it soon becomes clear that trying to identify key *gender* differences is a serious and more complex task than thinking about Mars and Venus might have led us to expect. It was easier when we could reduce everything to sex. This is partly because, in spite of the postmodern insistence that 'sex' is as much a construction as gender, sex is a much easier category to work with than gender. Genetic, chromosomal, reproductive and anatomical factors are all easy to identify and examine. We can see the differences in chromosomes by looking through the microscope. It is far harder to isolate gender factors in any detailed way because of their close relation with other cultural factors such as ethnicity, region, class, temperament and age. In fact when we look at any set of differences, we do not always know what script we are reading. In trying to understand masculinity, for example, we have to recognize that there are other features which complicate the picture. Men from different cultures may diverge more greatly in how they react to a situation than a man and a woman from the same culture.

I saw an illustration of this some years ago when I was at a gathering of international students in Britain. I watched with great entertainment as two men, an Arab and an American, tried to hold a conversation with each other. In order for the Arab to have a decent conversation with the American he had to stand very close to him, so he might speak comfortably in a low, intimate voice. But the American felt invaded by this kind of proximity. He needed space, distance, autonomy, safety, so he stepped backwards and resumed his louder conversational style. The Arab looked puzzled, stepped forward, and tried to close the space to something more familial, close and congenial. The American looked anxious and stepped back again. Then, slowly, step by step, the Arab manoeuvred the American right across the room as each of them tried to find an appropriate distance from which they could comfortably conduct their conversation with each other. The combination of gender and ethnic factors was very evident, but how would we evaluate which of these characteristics was due to gender, and which to ethnicity?

Specific gender differences can also be difficult to identify because they are part of a cluster of cultural attitudes which change over time. When we are trying to give some sort of shape to the concepts 'masculine' and 'feminine' we also have to recognize that these are in a constant process of flux. In the early 1980s for example, the British firm Mothercare published a sales catalogue with a cover that would have been not only inappropriate but unthinkable in my father's generation. It was of a man with a naked chest holding the naked bodies of twin babies. The representation was clearly 'masculine' rather than 'feminine', the twins were not held inwards, towards the breast, but were looking outward, towards the viewer, free to gaze, but with the security of a man's arms around them. The constructed meaning of the image was clear: good fathers are those who offer both protection and intimacy to their offspring, and Mothercare is on the side of good fathers. The catalogue was an enormous success, and the items of babycare enjoyed an increase in sales. Yet it was a conception and a posture that would not have been acceptable as appropriate for a man in a previous generation. Who responded to the catalogue? It was, of course, women, for although the picture signified father-hood, the target group was mothers. Mothers saw in this an icon of a father 'bonding' with his children and embraced it as a positive image for relationships in their own families. Thirty years earlier it would have been regarded as offensive or even ridiculous, but it was now the epitome of sensitive masculinity and sold baby products. Ten years later the Mothercare image would probably not have had such success, and might have even become problematic again, as widespread incidents of child sexual abuse became much publicized in the country. The category of gender is a responsive category: it changes in relation to other ideas or attitudes in both personal and public domains. Some argue that the breaking down of differences in gender attitudes between younger men and women is very thorough in areas of body images and sexual behaviour.[11] Yet in the public domain there is always more caution.

So we have to acknowledge that there is a multiplicity of factors which combine to shape and interpret gender differ-ences at any particular time. At this level the postmodern decontructionists are saying something crucial: if we 'reify' gender and regard it as something fixed and definitive in the nature of relationships, we misunderstand it. We have to recognize that what is sometimes spoken of as gendered behaviour is not simply gender-related, but an interplay of many different social constructions. Furthermore, since the gender that we are interested in is attached to people, we cannot

---

[11] Kate Fillion, *Lip Service*.

ignore the interplay between gender characteristics and those of temperament or personality styles. Without acknowledging all of this, we stay in the business of simply reinforcing stereotypes.

Feminist Research into Difference

Thankfully, we do not have to rely on the mass paperback market for our understanding in this area. Over the last two decades, key work has been done in the area of relationships by competent researchers. Although their approach is a long way from the philosophical analysis of Irigaray and Brandotti, it is also in a different league from *Why Men don't Iron* or *Men are from Mars, Women are from Venus*. Most of these are academics who, in a way similar to some of the feminist writers of the 1960s, have also made their own work accessible to a popular audience. These scholars include those who write in the areas of psychology, therapy, sociology and linguistics. The psychologists have produced a considerable portfolio of work over the years. Carol Gilligan was comparing diverse traits in the psychology of men and women in the early 1980s when many feminists were reluctant to consider them. Nancy Chodorow and Lillian Rubin were looking at male-female differences along post-Freudian lines, but trying to explain them in developmental rather than sexual-biological terms.[12] Their work has influenced a generation of therapists. Lynne Segal has done pivotal work in sociology, especially in the sociology of masculinity. Her work is acknowledged by people of many other disciplines around the world.[13] These writers all have

---

[12] Carol Gilligan, *In a Different Voice* (Cambridge, MA: Harvard University Press, 1982), Nancy Chodorow, *The Reproduction of Mothering* (Berkeley: University of California Press, 1978); Lillian Rubin, *Just Friends: The Role of Friendship in our Lives* (New York: Harper and Row, 1985) and *Intimate Strangers* (Glasgow: Fontana, 1985).

[13] Lynne Segal, *Slow Motion: Changing Masculinities, Changing Men* (London: Virago, 1990.) See David Tacey's acknowledgement of her work in, *Remaking Men: The Revolution in Masculi* (Melbourne: Viking, 1997) pp. 9, 15.

strong feminist sympathies, and feel that women's lives can only be improved by engaging with differences rather than assuming sameness. All this work has been significant in helping us to explore and identify differences, whilst refusing the conclusion that men and women cannot be any other way. In many areas of thinking, what they have said has almost become the new orthodoxy.

Another key contributor is socio-linguist Deborah Tannen, Professor of Linguistics at Georgetown University, Washington DC, whose research has been presented in two books which have become best-sellers. Tannen was McGraw Distingished Lecturer at Princeton when she published *You Just Don't Understand*, and her work is built on the starting point that although they are different, women and men have equally valid conversational styles. In her preface she explains why, in spite of her intention, some women remain suspicious of the emphasis on difference. She echoes the fears that Jean Joseph Goux has expressed, although more concretely:

> Some women fear, with justification, that any observation of gender differences will be heard as implying that it is women who are different – different from the standard which is whatever men are. The male is seen as normative, the female as departing from the norm. And it is only a short step – maybe an inevitable one – from difference to 'worse'.[14]

Tannen is very aware that the bid for equality has held previous feminist scholars back from considering and naming differences. She is in sympathy with 'those who wish there were no differences between women and men – only reparable social injustice'.[15] She has little time for biological essentialism, placing her own emphasis clearly in the cultural category. She also sees the dangers of reductionism whenever women and men are divided into two categories and generalisations are given. So, given all these reservations, why then has

Deborah Tannen, *You Just Don't Understand: Women and Men*
Conversation (London: Virago, 1992) pp. 14–15.
Id. p. 15.

she opted for 'difference' in her own analysis of gender communication? Her answer is very straightforward: because difference is there. Denying it can 'only compound the confusion that is already widespread in the era of shifting and re-forming relationships between women and men'.[16]

It has not only been feminist writers who have been keen to look at differences whilst developing critiques of essentialism. Although it was clearly in women's interests to attack bad theories, particularly ones which left women with so few practical options, male scholars have also moved into the area. This was not merely to show solidarity with women, but also to engage with their own agendas in various studies of masculinity. Similar questions about identity and gender relations have become the subject of a number of studies by men who are psychologists, social scientists, and theologians. Stuart Miller writes a book on male friendship, Robert Bly invites men to be initiated anew into the world of the father, Reuben Fine tries to get men to rediscover the forgotten male psyche and Roy McCloughry examines masculinity from a Christian perspective. The resulting volumes are diverse in a similar way to the studies done by women writers. Australian psychologist David Tacey notes this in his book *Remaking Men*. He argues that there is now a widening gulf between the feminist-influenced 'critical' writing which seeks to destabilize patriarchal masculinity, and the Jungian-inspired 'popular' writing which seeks to promote a 'new-old' masculinity. He is profoundly critical of the traditional biological reductionism, present in much Jungian orthodoxy, and expressed in his example, by Monick:

> Males and females are significantly different anatomically and biologically. It is my assumption that from these differences certain distinctions have evolved into the psychological characteristics of masculinity and femininity. The characteristics are gender-specific since their basis is biological: they are instinctual and archetypal.[17]

---

[16] Ibid. p. 16.
[17] Eugene Monick, *Castration and Male Rage* (Toronto: Inner Books, 1991) pp. 11–12.

He feels it is time to leave this behind and to 'remake masculinity'. Not least, there is the need 'to differentiate the new self-esteem from the old masculinist arrogance, to separate the new happiness from the old complacency, to tell the differences between human rights and patriarchal privileges'.[18]

Differences in Relationship and Friendship Patterns

In these studies in sociology, psychology or socio-linguistics the most reliable research has yielded a surprising level of agreement on what constitutes the key differences in the way men and women function and relate. Without trying to apportion 'weightings' to various cultural or genetic factors, various descriptions and analyses of difference recur. Broadly summarising, men and women are said to demonstrate different ways of interacting, expressing emotions, playing games, having a conversation, handling authority, giving and receiving instructions, initiating friendships, reacting to problems, establishing connections, relating to hierarchies, appraising situations and taking control. Sometimes, this is all seen as evidence that men and women orientate themselves 'differently towards reality'. Men are more likely to be separate individualistic, oppositional, thinking in terms of binaries, whereas women show greater 'connectedness' and orientate themselves empathetically towards others. This is a conclusion similar to that of Luce Irigaray and Hélène Cixous, although with different philosophical underpinnings.

It is interesting to examine some of these differences by looking, for example, at some of the studies on friendship. It is generally suggested that men have much greater difficulty in forming intimate relationships than women. This conclusion is reinforced by Stuart Miller in his study of male friendship in America. He suggests that 'Men may have wives, they may even have women friends, but their relationships with other men are generally characterised by thinness, insincerity, and

---

avid Tacey, *Remaking Men*, pp. ix and 14–15.

even chronic wariness.'[19] Another writer suggests that relationships between men 'do not call for high levels of self-disclosure nor its reciprocal – trust'. Consequently, 'female friendships are both more exclusive and more emotionally committed than male friendships'.[20]

Now that there are many men's groups, specifically committed to exploring male friendships, it is fruitful to look at the evidence they produce. Individual stories can illustrate a more general point. One author, a good friend of mine, had been part of a group which had worked at developing relationships which were non-competitive and emotionally open, and documented how complex this had been. He tells of an incident which took place after one member of the group had been brought back to emotional health after a period of breakdown. This man and my friend were walking to their cars when the man stopped, looked full into the face of my friend and told him: 'I just want you to know that I love you.' In spite of all they had done together in the group, my friend said that the hairs on the back of his neck stood up and a great shiver ran down his spine, and muttering something fast he made his escape. On the phone afterwards, we talked about how different the reaction might have been if that incident had occurred between two women. I mused about how as a woman I would have responded. I was fairly sure that I would have not felt at all threatened by such a disclosure of love; I didn't believe I would have feared it as a sexual overture, or felt my 'ego boundaries' had been invaded. In fact my response would have most likely been to give a warm hug to the woman who was sharing her feelings, to be emotionally moved, maybe shed a few tears, and for us both to feel how wonderful it is to have friends!

With multiple examples of this, it is now generally accepted as a truism in most studies of men and women that whereas

---

[19] Stuart Miller, *Men and Friendship* (San Leandro, CA: Gateway Books, 1983).

[20] Quoted in Julia Wood and Christopher Inman, 'Engendered Relations: Interaction, Caring, Power and Responsibility in Intimacy' in Steve Duck (ed.), *Social Context and Relationships* (Newbury Park, CA: Sage Publications, 1993) p. 234.

women relate easily to each other around experiences and feelings, male friends find it difficult to give or receive intimate self-disclosure. They connect more easily around impersonal issues, like ideas, sport, work, politics.

One characteristic method of researching differences in friendship patterns is to ask married men and women to name their six best friends. Inevitably the women find it difficult to write down the names of six friends, but that is more usually because they would rather put down seven or eight, and they have to do some negotiating in order to decide who to leave out. Husbands might be included on the list, but their omission would not be making any negative point. The men find the task difficult because they usually do not have six friends to name, and their wife might feature as the first (and sometimes only) name on their list.[21] Now, why do these differences occur? And if what Miller says is true, what is the explanation for the 'thinness and wariness' of male friendships in cultures of North European origin?

Explaining Difference

Some writers link it to differences in attitudes towards vulnerability. Whereas woman have the emotional space to show vulnerability, men do not. In them it is perceived as inappropriate weakness. Yet it is now acceptable for a man to express his vulnerable feelings to a woman, but still danger-ous for him to show vulnerability to another man. And since close friendship cannot develop between people who are guarded and covered with protective layers, it is clearly easier for women to develop close relationships than men. But naming a fear of vulnerability is simply to offer another symptom, not an explanation. And it begs the further question, what lies behind that?

Another answer relates it to the development of gender culture in the public and private arenas. Men have been segregated into work patterns and work environments where they have been required to be competitive, successful and

---

[1] See Rubin, *Just Friends*.

individualists. (And as psychologists tell us regularly, 'competing isolated egos do not easily open up their hearts to each other'.)[22] On the other hand, women have been given permission to spend more time with children and out of competitive work. So they can share their emotions, vulnerability and weaknesses with other women with relatively little loss of face.

But the differences in relationship are evident even before men and women ever enter the workforce. I had a chance to observe in practice early stages of male-female friendship patterns when I used to wait for my three sons to come home from school. Often if it was sunny, and my pre-schooler wanted to see his oldest brother playing. I would arrive early, during the mid-afternoon break and watch the different activities of the girls and the boys. Although there were some changes over the many years I spent standing at school gates, some things remained very much the same. When the play space was not segregated, the youngsters making most of the noise and creating most of the activity were inevitably boys. They would be hurtling around the playground chasing various shapes of ball, usually arguing about who was 'offside', who should pass the ball to whom, whether a goal had been scored, and who was winning. Nothing ever seemed to be obvious: all of these were opportunities for disagreement. The boys who were not involved in the big communal activity which took up so much space in the yard, were often isolated. They were very much on their own and looked out of it. Some girls were involved in running, but their games were more likely to be less rough and noisy: skipping was popular (when this was in fashion) and there they all had a 'turn'. More likely, however, they tended to go around in small groups or in twos. Girls had 'best friends' and the way they expanded their circle was often to run up to a third girl and say, 'Do you want to share a secret?' or, more inquisitively, 'Do you know a secret?'. The sharing of the secret would allow a third or fourth person into the intimacy. It would be creating a bond, a closeness, and something they would then continue. Not that

---

[22] Jim Olthuis, *Keeping our Troth* (New York: Harper & Row, 1986).

this intimacy was always cosy. Sometimes I would notice a new constellation of girls, with a former 'best friend' now isolated. As the girls ran to me, a regular landmark, to share their news (Charlotte had a new baby brother, grandma had moved house, Petra had a birthday), I would ask 'but what's the matter with Lisa?' The answer was often a kind of denial, 'Oh , she doesn't want to play.' And Lisa's former best friend would run off, with her arm tucked in another's, whispering conspiratorially. Boys were as ready to cut others out too and usually in a much more overt way, often decided by physical features ('he's too slow to be on the team', 'too little to be in goal'), but much of their activity was subject to the larger objective, rather than to their own relationships with each other. The boys on the receiving end of the 'shut out' also found girls were unlikely to respect them either.

Pushing gender differences further and further back into childhood makes it difficult to argue that the causes are to be found in an adult cultural context. Some writers, particularly Chodorow and Gilligan, have suggested that we would have to go a long way back to understand the power and force of these differences. Women and men are oriented in different ways towards reality because there is some patterning in their very psyches which draws them in these directions.

However, even though Chodorow would argue for differences at this very basic level, she would not buy into any part of essentialist biology. Arguing from attachment theory, she links these differences of orientation not to anatomy but to psycho-social development. She maintains they are related to the emotions which occur early in the conscious/unconscious development of small children. Especially significant is a boy's need to 'separate' from his mother, to find his own emotionality and sexuality, which a girl, being the same sex, does not need to do.

In the formation of identity there are said to be two key processes: bonding and detachment. Both girl and boy children experience attachment to the mother, as the primary care-giver. But the main way a girl can acquire a sense of herself is by continuing the attachment or bonding with her mother who in turn identifies with her daughter. As a result girls grow up with their primary definition of self permeated with a basis of empathy. Being feminine means being and feeling connected to others; ego boundaries are fluid and permeable. For a boy, however, the process is different. In order to develop his identity as a man he needs to relinquish his bonding and attachment to his mother, for, being different from her, he cannot identify with her. So a boy's gender identity is created by emotional separation.[23] His ego boundaries are more fixed and definite, and he has to work out his own identity in relation to his father, which is why fathering is such an important activity with reference to sons. Consequently as adults, men fear closeness for it threatens their sense of separate identity, while women fear isolation and aloneness for it threatens theirs. Carol Gilligan sums it up: 'Since masculinity is defined through separation while femininity is defined through attachment, male gender identity is threatened by intimacy while female gender identity is threatened by separation.' According to Gilligan, women speak in unison 'in a different voice'. Women's concerns involve empathising and showing care, whereas men's concerns are based on abstract principles of justice and fairness.[24]

This has implications in many areas of male-female relationships. For example, there are differences in what men and women say they most dislike about each other's attitudes. Women may dislike not being shown respect and feel indignant, but men may experience it as a crisis of identity. Men are also more likely than women to be highly sensitised in this area and to interpret certain responses as a 'put down'. This reflects too in intimate relationships. Most men feel annoyed if their sexual advances are rebuffed, whereas for a woman the distress comes when she does not feel 'cherished'.

The separateness/connectedness divide is very significant in intimacy and sexual expression. Many have pointed out that for many men with strong ego-boundaries, emotional closeness is relatively hard to come by. Often then, sex is the only permissible route available to emotional warmth and expression.

---

[23] Nancy Chodorow, *The Reproduction of Mothering*, p. 167.
[24] Carol Gilligan, *In a Different Voice*, p. 8.

Consequently, because men may experience sex as the main part of the tenderness, in the lives of many men deep feelings themselves become sexualised, where affection, protectiveness and feelings of gratitude are often entangled together with sexual attraction. For most women differentiation is much easier because they have traditionally been allowed a wider range of emotional responses and expressions. Consequently, many women need emotional warmth and affection before they can commit themselves sexually, whereas many men feel that they need sex before they can let go of their other inhibitions and draw close. This means that within marriage itself where a man finds it difficult to be demonstrative or emotionally in tune with his wife, sex can be the way in which he expresses all his affection and love for her. This can present itself as a problem for women for whom emotional closeness is usually pre-requisite to full sexual enjoyment.[25]

Difference has its Contemporary Critics

Needless to say, those who embrace strong concepts of difference, not least both Gilligan and Chodorow, have their critics.[26] Some challenge their whole process of theorising. Arguing from some alleged pre-theoretical attachment crisis produces a thesis that is simply untestable. How do we *know* that boys face this problem of separation which results in such strong psychical factors? We are simply reading it back from currently observed criteria. Others point out that this is yet another form of essentialism, and one not far from the bio-logical reductionism it is trying to replace. What does it matter whether 'difference' has its origin in sexual difference, or in sexual difference which leads to a difference of emotional attachment to mother? Surely, either way, sex still lies at the bottom of it? And when we give such a significant role to

[25] Elaine Storkey, *The Search for Intimacy* (London: Hodder & Stoughton, 1995) p. 197.
[26] Christina Hoff Sommers, *Who Stole Feminism? How Women Have Betrayed Women* (New York: Simon and Schuster, 1994).

biology, to then 'explain' gender differences in relationships in terms of attachment theory is simply an 'add on'.

Others blame these theories for romanticising female empathy and connectedness, which always seems to give women the moral high ground and always sees men as ineffectual relaters.[27] The terms of the debate are already loaded, argues Kate Fillion, who challenges the identification of disclosure with intimacy:

> Men who say they demonstrate affection by doing things for others typically get low ratings on intimacy scales, women who say they demonstrate affection by telling others about their feelings get high ratings. Men tell researchers that they do feel close to their friends, and show it through 'mutual give and take' 'helping each other out', 'being there for each other' and sharing 'actiivites'. Not good enough many experts say: only mutual self-discloure counts as real closeness.'[28]

Her book attempts to refute notions which have become vogue, and she simultaneously attacks the popular and scholarly writings for propagating ideas of differences and thereby downplaying both similarity and equality. She refuses the 'truisms' that 'women love, men lust; women want relationships, men fear intimacy; women are nurturing, men are aggressive.'[29] She believes that women collude in perpetuating their own powerlessness and unhappiness when they push out theories that men and women are psychological opposites. Her own conclusion is that we must continue to do what we have been doing for thirty years: debunk the old gender myths which reinforce inequality and resist the new myths that 'we are more-than-equal when it comes to caring, sharing and keeping the peace, and we are more spiritual than sexual in the boardroom, the bedroom and every place in between.'[30] It seems that equality and sameness are not yet moribund, not even in psychology.

---

[27] Kate Fillion, *Lip Service*.
[28] ibid. p. 17.
[29] ibid. p. 338.
[30] ibid. p. 17.

In spite of these important points of criticism, the Chodorow thesis cannot be dismissed altogether. Locating 'difference' in our emotional development may not be testable in a positivistic sense, yet it does offer a useful framework for understanding some of the factors about male-female relationships which are otherwise inexplicable. And it is different from a bald biological reductionism in that it gives much space to other factors and scope for change; incorporating fathers into detailed early infant care, for example, would make 'separation' from mother much less of a crisis for the male psyche. But, like any theory, it is partial, and the full story remains to be told.

Gender and Communication

If the work of psychologists on difference raises such strong objections, the work of socio-linguist, Deborah Tannen, has met with very wide approval. That is partly because her style is non-judgemental and linked less to psychological theory than to a broad idea of gender culture. For Tannen, boys and girls grow up in different worlds of words. Boys relate to groups that are hierarchically structured, girls to friendship pairs. These differences provide the context in which men and women learn to listen and talk. Tannen's writing has different philosophical justifications from the work of the other theorists. Her approach is more empirical; she offers observations, stories of male-female communication, and then an interpretative reading. Her work is successful because many couples are able to relate it to their own communication patterns.

Her basic premise, that gender culture deeply affects how we learn to communicate, can be easily tested. I was brought up in post-war Yorkshire and much of my early experiences of conversation were gained by listening to my mother and her sisters. One of them would begin to talk on entering the house and removing her coat, and her brief 'solo' would be punctuated by interruptions and agreements until at some stage or another they would all be talking at once. I learnt from the age of about four that it was extremely discourteous to allow someone to finish a sentence. You had to finish it for them, or interrupt, just to show that you were listening. Throughout my young adulthood, communication was always a group activity, accompanied by noises of affirmation, grunts of support, exclamations. Empathetic listening was the most crucial ingredient in any discourse. Consequently, when I married Alan – a man, and from the South of England – the silence surrounding our conversations was a culture shock. In our first few months I would constantly be asking, 'Are you listening to me?' His measured response was, 'Yes, that is why I am not talking'.

Tannen builds up dozens of examples of the way in which men and women have different expectations in conversation. It is not only that men give and receive information and women relate empathetically, there are also differences in the way we read tones, gestures, intentions. Both men and women listen 'beneath' the conversation, but pick up different things. Men are more likely to pick up condescension, and women are more likely to hear anxiety or concern. Because so much of their own conversation is goal-related and functional, men may also be hard pressed to 'understand' much of women's conversation, and sit there waiting for them to 'get to the point'. But for women, the conversation *is* the point.

With these and a host of other differences, women and men can simply miss each other in communication and not know why the other seems frustrated. For example, I thought communication in our own marriage had greatly improved as time went on, which is why it came as a surprise when after about twenty years of married life my husband pointed out that I hardly ever actually answered his questions. On that day we were expecting a visitor and I was travelling to lecture in Warwick. Alan had just asked me what time my lecture in Warwick began. I replied by pointing out that it would be very difficult to get to the lecture on time if I stayed for coffee with his visitor, for the train from Marylebone went only once an hour, and I couldn't afford to miss the early one. My husband said that as usual I hadn't answered his question. I denied it: I had given a perfectly good answer. He disagreed: I had made up a much more complicated question and answered that. He was right. After some thought I realized why. I couldn't believe he really wanted an answer to such a boring inquiry, so I went 'beneath' it to what I assumed was the real question, namely, could I stay to see the visitor and get to the lecture on time. I made the translation and produced the answer to the question which satisfied me, instead of simply supplying him what he had asked for. When he insisted he had simply been interested to know the time of my lecture, with no ulterior motive, I could not (and still cannot!) understand why. It simply seemed pointless information!

Summary

The contemporary interest in difference rather than sameness is not, for the most part, a return to pre-modern attitudes. To accept the existence of difference as a virtually incontrovertible fact, no longer entails buying into a biological essentialism. We can consider other sources. That is certainly true for postmodernity. But it is true also for those who are still working with a modernist metanarrative of justice and mutuality and exploring how equal relationships can best be achieved. The consensus seems to be that they have to be achieved without either abandoning or stereotyping differences between women and men.

The theorists in the social sciences all write from some philosophical assumptions, but few of them have explored any of the key theological questions implicit in the area. This is because most of the social sciences have developed from within a secularist framework for over a century, and they do not see much relevance for them in a study of theology. But it is also because theology has its own battles and has hardly led the way in advancing research in the area of sex and gender. In our next chapter we turn to some issues in theology and ask why not.

Chapter Six

From Social Science to Theology

If books on postmodern feminism are not widely sought after by the general public, books on academic theology have an equally limited audience. And yet, as in popular psychology, so in popular theology writings have proliferated in the area of sex and gender. Like their secular counterparts, they contain a jumbled confusion of perspectives. There is a difference, however. Most of these books claim to be offering 'Christian' insights: telling the truth about men and women as God has created them and designed them to be. Sadly, though, too many of them rehash old ideas based on biological essentialism plus gender stereotypes, but support this by quotations from the Bible. This, unfortunately, serves to reinforce the connection between Christianity and an unexamined pre-modernity in the eyes of many of their critics.

During most of Christianity's history, theological interest in issues of sexuality has been limited to the areas of sexual ethics, the doctrine of 'man' (Christian anthropology), or pastoralia. Even within these areas, gender has rarely been a separate part of the discourse. Usually it was subsumed under 'sex' or hidden under what some people called 'masculine headship'. There were rumblings of enquiry in earlier centuries as some female mystics tried to find a spirituality which addressed them specifically as women, and some branches of the church tried to develop a theology which was overtly inclusive of men and women. The Reformation provided a new impetus with its embracing concept of the 'priesthood of all believers'. But a full discussion of sex and gender was not to take place until the late twentieth century.

When it did come, it was not only issues in Christian anthropology, sexual ethics and pastoralia that were to be the focus. It was the whole process of theologizing itself. For the key question in this new critical theology was not about finding a space for a discussion of sex and gender within the existing discourse. Rather, it was whether theology itself was an irretrievably gendered discipline, where all the language, concepts, arguments and assumptions were inherently masculine.

The Theological Context

Before we move into this current debate we need to step back and see it in in relation to the structure and history of theological enquiry. For, as an academic discipline, theology has had a much longer history than the social sciences, which did not come on to the scene until after the Enlightenment. Until the entrenched secularism of the late twentieth century, the study of theology had always been an integral part of the curriculum of western education. Not that it was ever simply seen as just another academic discipline as it had never regarded itself as a neutral or objective science, for example, in the way in which some scientists and mathematicians used to claim objectivity for their disciplines. Now, of course, it is widely conceded that even in the most rigorous of scientific areas there are axioms and assumptions of a fundamental philosophical nature which provide a starting point for the very analysis and accumulation of knowledge. This issue is not very remarkable for theologians. For Christian theology has always been fairly overt about its starting point, which is that the meaning of life, if there is one, lies beyond the boundaries of most of our sensory knowledge and experience. I say, 'if there is one' because today many contemporary theologians are happy to do their theology without addressing the vexing question of whether they believe it or not. (This came home to me in a discussion once with some theologians who trained people for Christian ministry. When someone asked if we could formulate, as a working document, a statement of faith to which we might assent, this was met with embarrassment. When two reluctant colleagues were pressed for some credal affirmation, one of them offered tentatively, 'I can say, I hope there is a God.')

By and large, theology has been built on more than vague hope that there is a God; it has proceeded from the tacit, but widespread acknowledgement that if indeed God exists, then we have some obligation to know something about God. We also need to consider the question as to whether human life itself can be understood except in relation to God. For those reasons alone, as well as for the historical and literary interest of the material, the study of biblical texts, doctrine and history is deemed to be important. They give us both a way of understanding the nature of faith and the content of what Christians believe. This does not mean, however, that the study of theology has ever been a simple task. On the contrary, a large number of philosophical perspectives, historical influences, traditions and interpretations have always been part of the development and shape of the discipline. Each of these in turn has left some legacy on the contemporary theological discussion of sex and gender.

Scripture and Tradition

The central focus of Christian theology has been the Christian Scriptures, the Old and New Testaments. Yet theologians are not simply biblical exegetes. They investigate what some generally refer to as the 'Tradition of the Church', grappling with issues of history, philosophy doctrine and canonical authority in the context of the historic creeds and councils. There is an ongoing question in theology about the relation between tradition and Scripture, a question that is both subtle and intricate. Some argue that Scripture cannot be seen except as a part of tradition, and subject therefore to tradition (which in Catholicism usually means the *magisterium*) for its interpretation. For what are the Scriptures other than those books ratified by a council of the early Church? 'Tradition' first drew up the Canon and decided what constituted the Holy Bible. It was within the tradition, from the Church Fathers onwards, that the doctrines of the Church were first articulated in its creeds, catechisms and confessions. The Nicene Creed, the Thirty Nine Articles, the Westminster Confession, the Heidelberg Catechism, and all the other historic formularies which contain the basic affirmations of what Christians believe, are not found in Scripture but are the products of the Church's reflection on Scripture which then become embedded in our theology.

Others insist that the Scriptures themselves are the yardstick for tradition. The Canon might have been ratified by men, but the books in the Canon were inspired by the Holy Spirit of God as the touchstone for our faith. The creeds articulate the teachings of the biblical Christian faith in summary form. Tradition itself has to be held up against the teachings of Scripture to ensure that orthodxy prevails. That is how we develop concepts of orthodoxy and heresy. Heresy is the name given to any tradition which departs from biblical teaching and which therefore cannot be regard as authentic. What the councils of the Church have always done, whether at Jerusalem, or Alexandra, Nicea, Geneva or Heidelberg, is to look at what has become embedded as Tradition and ask if this is truly biblical. Where error has crept in, it has been necessary to revise it and re-present it to the Church.

Philosophy

The study of theology is also affected by other philosophical perspectives and assumptions which have travelled through the centuries. Philosophy has always played a major role in theology, even though the extent of that influence may be unacknowledged or even unrecognized. The impact of Greek philosophy (which itself was influenced by a pagan culture) has been felt in theology for two thousand years. The legacy of the debate between the Platonists and the Aristotelians has passed down through the centuries and is found in churches today, so that people in the various churches who may never have read either Plato or Aristotle could still be affected by them in their own understanding of the faith. Similarly, Kantian idealism, Cartesian dualism, British empiricism,

Hegelian antithesis, utilitarianism, European existentialism, and even the works of Ludwig Wittgenstein have all impacted on the way that we approach theology today. The *Sea of Faith*, for example, is a product of its time; it could only have come at the end of the second millennium.

Culture and Context

Finally, other prevailing cultural ideas also make their impact on the study of theology. The Scriptures were themselves given into specific cultures and are read today in other cultures, and there is always a process of weighing what is contemporary significance. The culture of our societies provides both the context in which we think about God and also the material conditions through which we think about God. Current societal values will play into our theologizing and what we deem to be significant or appropriate discourse. Theology in Britain in the seventeenth century needed to relate to the beginnings of modern science in a way that was different from theology in North Africa in the third century. Latin American liberation theology comes out of the twentieth century not out of Britain in the fifteenth, even though the same biblical texts were available at both times.

In some particularly conservative colleges of theology there is such understandable wariness about the extent to which 'external' influences have dominated the development of theology that the discipline itself is often approached with suspicion. Some theologians are concerned that theology has become sterile, dry, formulaic, involving too much spurious and academic debate. In an attempt to counter its potentially negative influence they choose to limit their own enquiry largely to biblical studies, systematics and ethics (which is seen as 'applied biblical studies'.) This way, it is felt, we can at least achieve some objectivity and definiteness as we ground our faith on a firm foundation and agreed basis of authority. Yet this retreat can be dangerous. It hides the fact that we can never escape our own human limitations and our cultural and historical location. For when the biblical texts themselves have to be read, understood and applied within a context which is inevitably different from the contexts into which they were first given, there is inevitably some process of interpretation and extrapolation. Even the most pious or scholarly of us should beware of the over-confidence that insists they can always grasp and present the truth without any kind of error.

Reading the Bible

We therefore never read Scripture 'neutrally'. We always bring to the biblical text our own minds, our own perspectives, ideas, attitudes, location, history, culture, nuances and concerns which are all, themselves, extra-scriptural. We also absorb biblical teaching in the context of our own embodied situation as persons, with regional, ethnic and gendered differences. There is nothing new about this. People have approached Scripture this way through the centuries, which is why the Bible has been such a powerful catalyst for cultural change. It can speak into every situation with challenges relevant for that time and location, nourishing movements for reform within church and society. Many have pointed out that a 'biblical worldview' lies beneath our seventeenth-century concept of law, our development of science, of political democracy, and of honest and accountable public service.

Yet because we approach the Bible from our different locations we can also find ourselves in disagreement. It is quite possible to be completely committed to faith in God and to reading the Scriptures yet still sometimes be trapped by our own philosophical assumptions of which we are unaware. So even when people agree that the Bible offers us truth they do not necessarily agree on what that truth is. We need to define and explore what we mean by truth for it sometimes has a historical referent, sometimes linguistic, or legal, propositional, parabolic, narrative, didactic, biographic or prophetic, all of which are modalities through which truth is received and understood). We can get it wrong. Our understanding, exegesis, interpretation and application of Scripture are, sadly, even amongst the best of us, prone to error, and that is inevitable, for in spite of our best efforts we, unfortunately, are not omniscient. We are not God. We are limited finite beings with finite human minds often imprisoned in very limited ways of understanding the world. For although God speaks truth into our human condition, our human condition means that we do not always receive it.

At this point it seems important to clarify what I am not saying. I am not offering this series of qualifications and cautions as a justification for either agnosticism or relativism. Nor am I suggesting that we are forever doomed to provisionality and approximation. Postmodernity is difficult to square with committed Bible study. I have no interest in siding with the 'liberal' claim that those who are committed to certainty are, *ipso facto*, arrogant and presumptuous. To hold on to a belief in the authority of a Creator God, the destructive power of sin, the atoning work of Christ and the empowerment of the Holy Spirit is not arrogance. It is to do nothing more than acknowledge the faith. I am not countering fervently held belief in any way, but simply pressing for a little humility. For humility has to be an essential ingredient in the task of theology. Like any students or scholars, theologians are servants, not masters (or mistresses) of what they study. It is important to recognize that once any of us claims infallible authority on biblical interpretation, then we have already ceased to see ourselves as human, and are now claiming divinity – being close to God, but only in an advisory capacity.

So we need to constantly examine the assumptions that we bring to any reading of the Bible, and some of those assumptions are related to sex and gender. For, in our striving to be biblical we may be merely cultural in off-loading some of the pervading, unexamined attitudes and ideas about the relationship between men and women, which we then unconsciously impose upon Scripture. This again is nothing new. Many of our biblical commentaries contain observations which we now know to be more related to prevailing cultural ideas than to the real teachings of Scripture. It is even the case that biblical translation itself can be affected, and in an attempt to make the text very clear, the result is as much an interpretation of the actual words, as a translation.

An obvious example of this comes in St Paul's letter to the Romans (16:1). He sends the letter with Phoebe, and urges the church to welcome her and give her warm recognition. Yet our translations deprive us of the full impact of what Paul says, for Phoebe is referred to in Greek as *'diokonos'* (without any feminisation of the ending), and in the next verse as *'prostatis'* (normally 'leader'). Yet, through the translation into English, she has been given for years the status 'servant of the church' and 'helper'. There may be some exegetical justification for this weaker translation of *prostatis,* but none for *diakonos.* Thomas Schreiner defends the translation rather lamely: '. . . many think that Phoebe is called a deacon in Romans 16:1. It should be noted, however, that the word *diakonos* . . . is often a general term and thus one cannot be sure that Phoebe was a deacon.'[1] The point is, however, the partiality of the translation. The translators have cut out certain meanings for us, and they have translated exactly the same word quite differently when it is used elsewhere. When Paul applies the word *'diokonos'* to his own calling, or when it is used to describe Timothy, the translators then give it the status of someone who has been set apart as a deacon, office-holder or, generally, minister. Why was this translation not used in Phoebe's case, even when Paul had generously included her in the same description of service that he applied to himself? Why, rather than being called simply 'deacon' is she called 'servant'? It can only be because the translators did not believe Paul meant it! They had to make sure it was understood that Phoebe, as a woman, could not possibly have been a deacon in the same sense as Paul or any other man. So they spoke for Paul, nailing down the meaning, and depriving us, incidently, of recognizing the courteousy and gratitude Paul accords to this woman's ministry.

So biblical studies may be 'safer' than theology, but reading the Bible still leaves us prone to the safe and philosophical assumptions that we brought to the study of theology.

---

[1] Thomas Schreiner 'The Valuable Ministries of Women in the context of Male Leadership' in John Piper and Wayne Grudem (eds.), *Recovering Biblical Manhood and Womanhood* (Wheaton: Crossway Books, 1991) p. 219.

The questions of sex and gender in theology occur therefore at several levels. They come at the level of tradition itself, where the past practices of the Church, its government, its leadership patterns and its liturgy have taken up positions on men and women which need to be addressed. They also occur at the level of Scripture. Are we basing our tradition – our practices and indeed our theology – on a wise interpretation of Scripture, or are we distorting the message in some way? They occur at the level of influences. How much do we take prevailing cultural ideas or arguments into our own mind-set (including ideas of biology and roles) and then overlay them with theological justification? Finally, they occur at the level of power and privilege. To what extent are decisions made by the 'powerful' or influential in the Church influenced by the very fact of their own power. And if they do, in what way is it different from any secular pattern of patriarchy? These are some of the questions behind the discussion which will occupy the next chapter.

Chapter Seven

Sex and Gender in Theology: From Pre- to Postmodernity

With the same caveats and qualifications that I offered earlier, I want to introduce Goux's distinction between pre-modern, modern and postmodern into the theological discourse on sexuality. The concept 'pre-modern' would characterise most of the discussion as it has been formed by the traditions of the Church. Certainly, one might say (as I suggested earlier) that there is an unavoidable 'pre-modernity' whenever one talks of our humanness as derivative. If we are brought into being by a Creator, and thereby dependent on that Creator for our existence, we have already come down on one side of the creation/ construction debate. Yet there is more to the pre-modern position than just believing that sexuality is put into the creation by God, for our sexuality can be given, and yet our 'differences' can be also developmental and cultural. But there is little acknowledgement of this in the pre-modern mentality.

Pre-modernity in a Theology of the Sexes

Many theological writers through the centuries saw difference as total, almost deterministic. It maps out our relative place in reality. It decides what God has created men and women for, recognizes what sins we are responsible for, determines what roles we may play, judges what gifts we may excercise. A pre-modern perspective in theology carries with it a welter of assumptions which interpret difference as all-embracing; it is the God-ordained structure of human identity, through which we are given our functions, feelings, place and perceptions. It even encompasses our spirituality.

There is no shortage of evidence for this. Any study of the early Church Fathers will unearth misogynous comments which show a great gap in the way men and women are perceived. Women are the ones mostly blamed for the evil of the world. The Fathers variously describe women as 'the devil's gateway',[1] 'misbegotten men',[2] or 'a temple built over a sewer'.[3] In a climate of asceticism, women's difference from men and their sexuality were deeply problematic. To put it bluntly, women's sexuality was a fundamental problem, a snare of the devil to draw men away from purity into lust. The austere St Jerome was so anxious about sexual difference that he urged his women followers to pursue a way of life that made them as unattractive as possible, to do penance and ensure that their difference could not be noticed. A truly spiritual woman would be 'squalid with dirt, almost blind with weeping . . . continence . . . her luxury, her life a fast'.[4] He also brought some of his anxieties about women's sexuality, even about its expression in marriage, into biblical exegesis itself, claiming an uncleanliness about anything that was 'coupled'. Anything that denoted female difference from the male, even the number two, was for Jerome profoundly threatening and therefore must illustrate God's own displeasure:

> There is something not good in the number 2 . . . while scripture on the first, third, fourth and sixth days relates that having finished the works of each God saw that it was good, on the second day He omitted this altogether, leaving us to understand that 2 is not a good number because it prefigures the marriage contract.[5]

[1] Tertullian, 160–220 AD, *On the Apparel of Women*, Book 1, chp. 1.
[2] Thomas Aquinas, *Summa Theologia*, Pt. 1, 4 Qxcii, art. 1, 2; Qxciii, art. 4.
[3] Clement of Alexandria.
[4] Jerome, Letter cxvii, quoted in Elaine Storkey, 'Spirituality and Sexuality' in D. Torrance (ed.), *God, Family and Sexuality* (Edinburgh: The Handsel Press, 1996) p. 140.
[5] Quoted by Jane Barr 'The Influence of St Jerome on Mediaeval Attitudes Towards Women' in Janet Martin Soskice (ed.), *After Eve* (London: Marshall Pickering, 1990) p. 96.

Although these worst excesses of a pre-modern mentality belong to history and not to contemporary Christianity, these attitudes have not altogether departed, either from biblical exegesis or from the attitudes of churchmen. In 1984 William Oddie wrote *What Will Happen to God?*, a book which gaves an apocalyptic vision of what would happen to Christian truth if fundamental differences between women and men are not heeded in our practices. He pictures a domino effect, where one piece (for example, the revision of gender-exclusive language) will topple the whole of the Christian edifice.

Oddie's book is littered with unexamined concepts, uninvestigated assumptions, and poor hermeneutics. His analysis leans heavily on secular stereotypes which sound so much like any secular book of pop psychology. He insists, for example, that 'modern industrial culture is one in which the male (with his generally greater aggression, 'goal-orientation', 'visual-spacial ability'. . .) is particularly suited'.[6] At the same time he lapses into piety when talking about women. For they are to 'protect the world and men like a mother, and purify life as the Virgin'.[7] In fact, women's difference not only disqualifies them from performing tasks which have traditionally fallen to men, including leadership in the church, it also puts them on a different religious plane. Oddie has some very odd things indeed to say about the relation between spirituality and sexuality. He makes the extraordinary claim that, 'It is a clear and consistent biblical assumption that . . . biological differences (of men and women) correspond to clear differences of spiritual identity.'

He attempts to substantiate this, however, not by reflecting on Scripture, but by offering the same point again as an anthropological explanation: 'In all societies, this perception of an essentially spiritual, as well as merely biological difference between the sexes has been reflected in a clear delineation of their social roles and in distinct ways of behaving.'[8]

The argument is hardly enhanced by its circularity. Here is a classical exposition of a pre-modern view of difference: fixed,

---

6 William Oddie *What Will Happen to God?* (London: SPCK, 1984) p. 69.
7 ibid. p. 70.
8 ibid. p. 33.

immutable, God-given. The whole of male-female reality is permeated by their differences which are reflected in biology, roles and spiritual identity. It is these differences which also bar women from the priesthood, for priests are representatives of Christ. But Christ was male. Therefore, quite simply, it is impossible for a woman to perform the priestly act as Christ's representative. They have the wrong kind of genitals. (There is a shift in concept here, of course, from what is needed to be Christ's 'representative', to being Christ's 'representation' (i.e. to look like him), but that usually gets lost in the passion of feeling.) One opponent of the ordination of women sums it up baldly, 'When men can have babies, women can be ordained.'

Although we are more likely to find these arguments offered from a more Catholic perspective, evangelicals often have views not too dissimilar. They would be more likely to suggest them, however, in the context of a biblical exposition. In 1970 the *Ladies Home Journal* was given an exegesis of Genesis 1:26–28 by a foremost evangelist, Billy Graham. According to Graham, the passage indicated that God had created a natural order for man and woman: 'The biological assignment was basic and simple: Eve was to be the child-bearer, and Adam was to be the breadwinner . . . wife, mother, homemaker -- this the appointed destiny of real womanhood.'[9]

Yet when one looks at the passage there is, of course, nothing at all there about breadwinning, childbearing or homemaking, and not a word about biology or destiny. The verses in Genesis are about something very much bigger, namely God's power in creating the human race, making male and female together in the 'image of God' and giving them the 'cultural mandate'. The passage is, in fact, extraordinarily inclusive. 'And God blessed *them*, and said to *them* "Be fruit-ful and increase in number". . .' (verse 28). Far from it being a handbook on *difference* this passage makes no differentiation between the man and the woman at all. They are allocated no different tasks, or distinct roles according to some differences

---

[9] Billy Graham, 'Jesus and the Liberated Woman', *Ladies Home Journal*, Dec (1970) p. 42.

in nature. They both receive identical instructions and are given the blessings of God.

So where does this exegesis come from? Not from Scripture, but from ideas already held in a particular cultural context about the roles of male and female, and although this author has no axe to grind, others over the last twenty years have made gender issues their mission. The long process of a consumerist, American, macho culture claiming the right to be *the* interpreters of Scriptural truth has produced an evangelicalism which is often nationalistic, right-wing and patriarchal. Yet this evangelicalism cannot see that its own assumptions are anything but biblical. All contributors are polarised into 'camps' and any subtleties or complexities of the gender debate are quickly lost. In contemporary publications we see gender concepts still being subsumed under sexual difference; we still read justifications of 'essentialism' which masquerade as biblical wisdom. In an article in 1991, for example, on 'Rearing Masculine Boys and Feminine Girls' we are solemnly warned about the dangers of fathers 'stepping into the vacuum' created by working mothers:

> In cases where the father does increase participation in child rearing, it has been suggested that the differences in the mother's and father's role in the family may become blurred as the father becomes involved in historically feminine roles. This may result in greater difficulty for children to distinguish between proper male and female roles.[10]

However, although this all sounds exactly like the pre-modern position I described earlier, there is a distinction. The key factor which constitutes male-female difference for most of these writers is not just nature, or biology. It is *authority*. At the heart of male-female relationships is a divinely decreed order of rule or sanction, the principle of 'masculine headship'. Variously interpreted as having operative jurisdiction throughout the whole of creation, or only in marriage, family and church relationships,

---

[10] Alan Rekers, 'Psychological Foundations for Rearing Masculine Boys and Feminie Girls' in John Piper and Wayne Grudem (eds.) *Recovering Biblical Manhood and Womanhood*, p. 304.

this is the difference which underlies all other differences between men and women, and because this principle is laid down
by God, it cancels out any other considerations which might
modify or contradict it. Take the important principle of 'equal
rights' for example. One author asks, 'Does a wife possess under God all the rights that her husband has *in an unqualified
sense?*' The answer is clearly no, for the man has authority over
the wife and his marriage. Indeed, he spells it out for us: 'The
ideal of "equal rights" in an unqualified sense is not Biblical.'[11]
(The implied concession that there might be some 'qualified'
sense of equal rights is, of course, misleading. Equal rights
which are 'qualified' are not equal.)

We apparently run into the same 'biblical' problem when the
men who are in authority decide to relax certain restrictions on
women:

> It seems clearly contrary to the apostle's teaching, for some to
> argue that the male elders in the church may give a woman the
> right to give the exposition of the Word of God to the church and
> to say that, since she does it under the authority of the male lead-
> ership, this activity would be acceptable. Paul rules out such an
> activity and underscores this by saying that in the public teaching
> situation where men are present, a woman must remain 'silent'
> with respect to this activity and not 'speak' (1 Timothy 2:12;
> 1 Corinthians 14:34–35).[12]

This means that even if they felt inclined to be inclusive, men
may not share their authority with women and listen attentively
whilst women use their gifts of communication. They may not
do this because they are men.

It is interesting, incidently, that even though the author here
is very sure about his position, he has come to it through less
than rigorous scholarship. When we consult the two passages
he quotes, we find he has compounded them together, even

---

[11] Raymond Ortlund, 'Male-Female Equality and Male Headship',
in John Piper and Wayne Grudem (eds.) *Recovering Biblical
Manhood and Womanhood*, p. 105.

[12] Paige Patterson, 'The Meaning of Authority' in Piper and Grudem
(eds.) *Recovering Biblical Manhood and Womanhood*, pp. 258–9.

though they are about different things. The passage in
Timothy does not make any reference to the 'public teaching
situation' and the word for 'teach' or 'explain' (*didaskō*) is one
which the New Testament itself uses with approval of a
woman (Priscilla in Acts 18:26). So whilst there is certainly a
prohibition here, it is specific to the situation, and cannot be
universal for all women. In Corinthians 14, the context is of
church worship but here the Greek word 'speak' does not
mean 'teach' but something altogether different. Paul is asking
that worship be orderly and dignified, not confused and noisy.
So the women should not interrupt the worship with 'chatter'
(or it could mean 'give ecstatic utterances'), but speak to their
husbands later, at home.

The various textual interpretations are not, however, the
key point. The crucial issue is what underlies the interpretations. It is the belief that women's nature decrees them as
different from men, and thus subordinate to men. Moreover it
is an insistence that this is sanctioned by divine *fiat*. God has
ordained it as a universal principle. Women are therefore
charged to respect the roles that God has assigned for men,
and not try to usurp them. Anything in the New Testament
which suggests some other perspective is argued away or
particularised. The position rests, as before, on an unyielding
essentialism. The difference is that it is now reinforced not just
by biology but also by theology.

Modernism in Theology and Gender

It is difficult to say when the 'modernist' reaction to the traditional position on male-female roles first came about. There
had certainly been Christian women writers and activists in
the 'first wave' of feminism in the nineteenth century who had
strongly questioned them. As they saw the injustices around
them the brief of these pioneers became a large one: everything
from suffragism to temperance was seen as part of women's
Christian concerns. There were much earlier periods in church
history also when people challenged the rigidity of the position
outlined above, and when women occupied more varied roles

in the church. But this was not 'modernity', just good biblical sense!

The modernity to which Goux refers is generally seen as being ushered in with the first writings in what is now called feminist theology. In 1960 Valerie Saiving Goldstein's article, 'The Human Situation: A Feminine View',[13] asked that religious studies which had previous considered only male experience should open themselves to consider distinctly female experience also. By the early 1970s a plethora of books, conferences and women's caucuses had grown up within the churches.

Hidden history of women

Some women theologians got to work on history, reclaiming women's hidden history in the story of Christianity. Biblical women – Mary Magdalene, Joanna, Susanna, Mary and Martha – all got new attention, along with those women with-out name whose stories were told in the Gospels. The women in the Acts of the Apostles suddenly came into their own: Junia the apostle, Priscilla, the teacher, the four prophet-daughters of Philip, Lydia the tradeswoman, along with Phoebe the deacon, and all the women listed in Paul's letters to the new Christians. Many women, concealed from view or silenced by time – scholars, matryrs, mystics, mothers, prophets, preachers and evangelists – were rediscovered, and brought out of the closets. We found fourth-century Monica, the mother of Augustine, Macrina sister to Basil, Gregory of Nyssa and friend to John Chrysostom, Blandina the early Christian martyr. In the old convents we discovered Hildegard of Bingen, Hilda of Whitby, Mother Julian of Norwich, Teresa of Avila. In the Reformation we found Augusta, Margaret Fell, the Quaker leader, women in the Tractarian movement. A century later the Ladies of the Scottish Covenant were heard again, their voices clear. The nineteenth century particularly came alive with women preachers and evangelists like Phoebe Palmer, the women in the abolition movement such as the

---

[13] Valerie S. Goldstein, *Journal of Religion* 40 (1960) pp. 100–112.

Grimké sisters, (Angelina and Sarah), Antoinette Brown, Sojorner Truth (a freed slave), Harriet Tubman, the Blackmore sisters, and women like Elizabeth Fry, Florence Nightingale, Josephine Butler, all active in social reform. For many of these pioneers, their involvement in the abolition movement in the United States and reform movements in Britain had drawn them into careful re-examination of the Bible, to test whether it could really be used to justify the restrictions placed on women.[14]

Whilst these women were simply retelling the stories, the modernist theologians were mounting their own attack on pre-modern notions of difference. Within many of the churches this was radical indeed, like 'picking up the ground on which we stand and shaking it'.[15] But the ground had to be shaken, and a firmer base found on which to stand. Weak arguments from nature had to be exposed. Rosemary Radford Ruether spelled it out:

> To put it bluntly there is no biological connection between male gonads and the capacity to reason. Likewise there is no biological connection between female sexual organs and the capacity to be intuitive, caring or nurturing . . . There is no necessary (biological) connection between reproductive complementarity and either psychological or social role differentiation. These are the work of culture and socialization, not of nature.[16]

Letha Scanzoni and Nancy Hardesty took up the same theme:

> Biology is not destiny and neither hormonal nor animal studies offer proof that human gender roles are innate. Rather they are assigned and reinforced through social learning. The meaning

---

[14] See Jennifer Fisher Bryant, *Lucretia Mott: A Guiding Light* (Grand Rapids: Eerdmans, 1996); Margaret Forster, *Significant Sisters: The Grass Roots of Active Feminism 1839–1939* (Harmondsworth: Penguin Books, 1984).

[15] Rosemary Radford Ruether, quoted in Letha Scanzoni and Nancy Hardesty, *All We're Meant to Be* (Grand Rapids: Eerdmans, 3rd edn., 1992) p. 121.

[16] ibid. p. 111.

and content of the labels 'masculine' and 'feminine' are totally determined by culture.[17]

All the old ideologies about a woman's place, roles, gifts, abilities were challenged and found wanting. Instead of *difference*, the focus shifted, as in equality feminism, to *similarity*. Women and men had so much in common, and suddenly, the modernist perspective found a strong, if unexpected echo in the traditional faith of the Church. For had not Christianity always recognized that men and women share a common humanity as the image of God, a common sinfulness as rebellious creatures, a common redemption in Christ who died for us, a common blessing in the gifts and outpouring of the Holy Spirit, and a common calling to faithfulness in the Kingdom of God? To move into a united sense of being male and female we needed to recover what had been missing so far: we needed to hear from women. 'Since being female is as much the predominant human experience as being male, the insights and experiences of women are as valuable as those of men.'[18] A theology that acknowledged our unity, and embraced the fundamental call to freedom and equality could indeed speak Good News into the lives of women.

Yet, for all the apparent solidarity of the original vision, there were different perspectives within theological feminism from the start. Many simply wanted greater liberty for women to be affirmed by the churches, not any revolutionary agenda. This meant, for them, reading the Bible faithfully and recognizing its radical message; seeing gender not as a series of legalisms and restrictions on women but as the faithful response of the Church to the freedom Christ brings. Exegetical analysis of dozens of key words – like ʿēzer, neged (helpmeet), ādām (humankind), kephalē (head), exousia, authenteō (authority) – as well as careful re-examination of the few problematic Pauline passages all brought new insights which did not support the restrictive position.

---

[17] ibid. p. 110.

[18] Ann Loades, 'Feminist Theology: A New Direction in Christian Studies', *Farmington Papers* MT10 (Oxford: Farmington Institute for Christian Studies, 1998) p. 1.

But other feminists were more sceptical about this procedure from the start. Their theology had a more fundamental
aim: to release women's experience as the *dominant*
hermeneutical tool, and free theology from the constraints of
its sexist past. For them the Bible was riddled with male
chauvinist attitudes, and too long in the service of patriarchy
to be any use in the liberation of women. In fact to the suggestion that the Bible could be effectively 'depatriarchalised',
Mary Daly mused what length such a 'Bible' might be. She
suggested there might be enough salvageable material to
provide an interesting pamphlet.

Feminist theologians – a broad church?

Out of these differences of emphasis, and also of belief,
feminist theology settled down into a number of different
nuances and positions. By definition they are not static. For
the very point of feminist theology is not to create new
systems. Its task is not systematic but episodic, to allow
theology to come from our midst. Yet, that these positions are
there is now incontrovertible. They vary in what they see to be
the key task of feminist theologizing, and in how they now
identify the Christian faith. For nothing is left as it was: all
fundamental questions of Christian doctrine, liturgy,
language and God have been re-examined. The aim, however,
was not so that feminists could come down on one side or the
other in the debate which has gone on through history, but so
that they could re-present the faith.

Nevertheless, camps have been formed, and now, feminist
theology encompasses a wide range of opinions, beliefs,
perspectives and attitudes. Some are 'equality theologians',
looking for ways of releasing the common gifts of women and
men. Others are, variously, liberation theologians, eco-
feminists, goddess feminists, women-identified feminists,
post-Christian feminists. Even the categories 'modern' and
'postmodern' tend to break down as the boundaries get
blurred. Some who begin with a modernist metanarrative of
equality sometimes slide into postmodern deconstruction even
without notice. Beneath all this is the question of what can

now be accepted as Christian revelation. Who speaks for God? One way of trying to understand feminist theology is to examine the answer to this question, for then the differences become evident.

The Bible as Canonical

When we raise the question about the status of the Bible, the first option is the one which offers fewest breaks with the past. Biblical feminists start from the acceptance that the Bible as passed down through the centuries is canonical – God's revelation to us. Yet they would insist that it has something to say to them personally as women, not just as adjuncts to men, or mediated through the *magisterium*. Culturally formed gender differences are no hindrance to God, for God searches out and speaks to women as they are.

Strictly speaking, however, biblical feminism is not part of a modernist reaction. Certainly it rejects the reductionism of pre-modernity and argues that culture, not biololgy, is the key to shaping and framing our gender roles. It discards the essentialist assumptions which are brought to the Bible and believes that the Scriptures support a retelling of the story of God's relationship with women, which cuts through most of the patriarchy of the past. It subjects the Bible to a rigorous study to understand its origins, its culture and the nuances evident in its human authors. It does not deny that the Bible also contains stories which can never be encouraging to women, those 'texts of terror', like the gang rape in Judges 19, which Phyllis Trible says cannot bring anything but sorrow for women. (For Trible, even these stories still have to be told, not with any hope of blessing, but simply 'in memoriam'[19] for those women who have been broken under patriarchy.) A biblical feminism acknowledges all these as crucial issues for women. Because of this, it incurs the wrath of many theological traditionalists who hit out at biblical feminism as if it were the enemy, with little understanding of the crucial work that is being done here.

---

[19] Phyllis Trible, *Texts of Terror: Literary-Feminist Readings of Biblical Narratives* (Philadelphia: Fortress Press, 1984) pp. 65–91.

Yet biblical feminists are at odds epistemologically with much of the rest of feminist theology. For they reject the primacy of women's experience as the interpretative framework with which we approach the Bible. For them, although experience is crucially important, it cannot be the standpoint from which we understand reality because the biblical text is communication from God, and cannot be subject to women's experience as some 'higher order' which ultimately arbitrates over it. Women's experience cannot itself have the last word. There has to be an intricate two-way relationship of experience and revelation, where our experience itself has to be examined and understood in relation to God and God's revelation about ourselves. Since the basis of our human identity is given, created by God, not simply constructed out of the particulars of our world, we have to be prepared to allow the depths of God's revelation to interpret us, and understand aright our worth and calling before God.

Perspectives which can more properly be described as part of the 'modernist' reaction, might include those of Elizabeth Schüssler Fiorenza, Judith Plaskow, Anne Carr, Elizabeth Johnson,[20] Sandra Schneiders and the early Rosemary Radford Ruether. I want to take two of those now as illustration.

A Canon outside the Canon
Fiorenza argues that feminist theology is a critical theology, born out of women's experience of misogyny. Because much of that misogyny is related to the way in which the Scriptures and tradition have been used we cannot simply identify canonical truth with the Bible as it has been traditionally received by the Church. The Bible has first to be subjected to critical scrutiny in which our 'hermeneutics of consent' must be withdrawn. Instead, a 'hermeneutics of suspicion' will lead us to see what has been left out, namely women's history, women's stories and women's participation in the development of faith. Women's difference from men has led to their being silenced and oppressed, even by Scripture itself:

---

[20] See Elizabeth Johnson, *She Who Is: The Mystery of God in Feminist Theological Discourse* (New York: Crossroad, 1992).

Because of its allegiance to the defeatedness in history, a feminine critical theology maintains that the hermeneutics of consent which understands itself as the actualising continuation of the Christian history of interpretation, does not suffice. Such a hermeneutics overlooks the fact that Christian Scripture and tradition are not only a source of truth but also of untruth, repression and domination. Since the hermeneutical contextual paradigm seeks only to understand the Biblical text it cannot adequately take into account the fact that the Christian past as well as its interpretation has victimised women.[21]

Old allegiances to the Bible therefore have to be challenged, not least the assumptions that the patriarchal texts of Scripture are in some way authoritative and an intrinsic part of the Word of God. And because the Bible cannot function as the main weapon in the political struggle for women's liberation, we need a new foundation. For Fiorenza this foundation is to be found in the *ekklēsia* of women: '(t)he hermenetical centre of feminist biblical interpretation is the women-church (*ekklēsia gynaikōn*), the movement of self-identified women and women-identified men in biblical religion.'[22]

This means, in effect, that Fiorenza offers us an alternative canon to that of Scripture. Her 'canon' is closer to home:

> The locus or place of divine revelation and grace is therefore not the Bible or the tradition of a patriarchal church but the *ekklēsia* of women and the lives of women who live the 'option for our women selves'. It is not simply 'the experience' of women but the experience of women (and all those oppressed) struggling for liberation from patriarchal oppression.[23]

In this 'canon outside the canon', we find that the real place of revelation is in the lives of women who live, and have lived,

---

[21] Fiorenza, *Bread Not Stone* (Boston: Beacon, 1984).
[22] Elizabeth Schüsser Fiorenza, 'The Will to Choose or Reject: Continuing our Critical Work' in L. Russell (ed.), *Feminist Interpretation of the Bible* (Oxford: Basil Blackwell, 1985) p. 126.
[23] ibid. p. 128.

authentic lives. Their stories do not have to be recorded in the
Scriptures or in the history of the Church; this is no process of
merely identifying 'role models'. It is much more that through
their struggling with hardship and suffering, they have refused
to bow the knee to patriarchy, and therefore in their lives and
communion we find the truth of who we are, and through that
process have a way of interpreting the rest of reality.

It is important to note that Fiorenza is not calling for a
rejection of the Bible or of the Christian metanarrative. Rather,
it needs to be interpreted aright because its message has been
ambiguous: 'the Bible is used against women in our liberation
struggle, and perpetuates alienation from ourselves and at the
same time has provided and still provides authorization and
visions for Christian women in our struggle against patriarchal
racism, sexism, classism and colonialism.'[24] So there is much in
the way the Bible meets the oppressed and brings freedom and
release that we need to hear. In this sense Fiorenza is closer to
the tradition of the Church than many other feminist theologians, recognizing what one writer has called, a 'liberative core
masked by centuries of misogyny'.[25] Fiorenza does not want to
relinquish the past completely. Where the Bible echoes the
liberation that we see in the lives and confessions of those who
bring the Good News, we can recognize that it is the truth of
God. Yet where it does not, it need have no claim on our
allegiance.

Although Fiorenza is part of the 'modernist' challenge to
theology, she also paves the way out of modernity, for in
locating revelation in the experience of women, she is
ostensively offering some universal concept as a hermeneutical
tool. Yet it is only *some* women who are the bearers of
revelation, only *some* experience that we need to start from,
and who makes the decision about the experience that counts?
There has to be a higher authority than women's experience to
decide what of all women's experience is the authentic core.

---

[24] Fiorenza, 'Roundtable Discussion: On Feminist Methodology',
Journal of Feminist Studies in Religion Vol. 1, No. 2 (1985) p. 75.
[25] Linda Hogan, *From Women's Experience to Feminist Theology*
(Sheffield: Sheffield Academic Press, 1995) p. 101.

Furthermore, when many different voices begin to be heard, when women's experience itself begins to splinter, it soon becomes difficult to retrieve any sort of universal base. In particular, feminist theology is accused of having a white, western, middle-class, elitist base. African-American 'womanist' theologians, Hispanic 'Mujerista' theologians, Korean Christian-shamanists all begin to insist that their own experiences and traditions are not recognized or addressed by white feminists. Equality and similarity are the wrong concepts. Difference becomes crucial. In the midst of all the challenges the door is open once again for postmodernity. There are many other feminist theologians who will go through it.

A Canon Within the Canon

Rosemary Radford Ruether is one of the most prolific feminist theologians. Her concerns are wide and include what would normally be categorised as church history, philosophy, language, eco-feminism, Christology, soteriology, religious experience, comparative religion. Her writings are voluminous and her position has gone through a number of stages, all of which makes her work difficult to summarise. At one level she shares the modernist commitment to equality, claiming that the 'egalitarian, counter-cultural vision is the true norm of Christianity'.[26] She also never quite leaves behind some version of essentialism or foundationalism, although sometimes where she sees her foundation to be is unclear:

> I would see Scripture as normative, not in the sense of infallible truths disclosed from beyond normal experience, or as unique experiences incomparable with other experiences, but rather as a foundational memory . . .[27]

---

[26] See here the discussion of Ruether in Francis Martin, *The Feminist Question* (Grand Rapids: Eerdmans, 1994) pp. 178–182, and Nik Ansell, *The Woman Will Overcome the Warrior* (Toronto: Wedge, 1994).

[27] Rosemary Radford Ruether, 'Is Feminism the End of Christianity?', *Scottish Journal of Theology* 43 (1990) p. 390.

Ruether has often been linked with Fiorenza, although the two are very different in their interests and their styles of writing. Like Fiorenza she begins with a basic belief in the retainability of the Christian tradition, whilst seeing the need to rid it of its androcentricity. Yet, unlike Fiorenza, Ruether did not initially look outside the Bible for an alternative locus of revelation in the liberation-experience of the community of women. She does not want to produce a dichotomy between tradition and experience. For her, that was not necessary. For what are Scripture and tradition other than 'codified, collective human experience'? And what is experience other than 'experience of the divine, experience of oneself, and experience of the community and the world'?[28] The Scriptures are the 'past experiences' of the community of believers, and the task for the contemporary believing community is to appropriate 'the foundational paradigm as the continuing story of its own redemption in relation to God'.[29] She recognizes, however, that this is difficult, because 'revelation is said to be closed and located in the past' and the faith has been codified and locked in so that the 'ongoing power of the Spirit sent by Christ to the community is no longer to "blow where it will" but is institutionalized in the authority of bishops'.[30] So God's real revelation must be released from the Scriptures and the Church to live again, and the 'authority of the official canonical framework overturned' so that the egalitarian vision can be realized.

Ruether therefore formulates her 'canon within the canon'. She takes the prophetic-messianic principle from the Scriptures and makes that her benchmark for true biblical faith. The call of the prophets away from injustice and idolatry, the bias to the poor and marginalized, the servant-leadership of Jesus of Nazareth, all fit with her understandings of the redemptive kernel of the Christian message. The new essentialism is not tradition, biology or Scripture, but justice for women.

---

[28] Rosemary Radford Ruether, *Sexism and God-Talk* (London: SCM, 1983) p. 12.

[29] ibid. p. 16.

[30] ibid. p. 124.

Therefore, the new hermenuetical principle has to be that: 'Whatever denies, diminishes, and distorts the full humanity of woman must be regarded as non-redemptive.'[31]

With this new interpretative framework, the whole biblical message now takes on a transformation, becoming itself a critique of injustice, oppression and patriarchy. Much of what has been accepted as legitimate practice in church history and contemporary Christianity is now seen as beyond the boundaries of a redemptive biblical hermeneutics. What is more, those texts of Scripture which were used to justify them can also be relegated to the rubbish bin. Only what is fully redemptive may remain.

Many questions remain about the method and direction of Ruether's work. In her later writings there seems to be a greater shift towards women's experience as having higher status as an interpretive tool. But one issue has been at the centre of most of the concerns of those Christians who have not been won over by the modernist critique. That is the person of Christ. If, as Ruether insists, revelation is not fixed or static but in a process of constant revision and response, where does that leave the notion that Christ is the unique revelation of God? And where does it place the death of Christ as the salvific redemptive act for the sins of the world?

Ruether tackles this in a number of writings. She sees the messianic principle demonstrated in the way Jesus takes on not kingship and domination, but humility. Jesus 'drastically reverses the social references of divine redemptive activity'. But to talk of Jesus as the *unique* representation of God would be misleading: it would also lead us back into all the problems of maleness which have so dogged the pre-modern tradition. 'Christ as redemptive person and Word of God, is not to be encapsulated "once for all" in the historical Jesus' but in the community of liberation today:

> This kind of spirit Christology does not separate out a past perfect historical Jesus from the ongoing Spirit. Rather it sees Christ as a

---

[31] Rosemary Radford Ruether, 'Theology as Critique and Emancipation from Sexism', p. 27.

power that continues to be revealed in persons, both male and female, in the present. Christ is located in a new humanity that discloses the future potential of redeemed life. The reality of Christ is not completed in the past but continues to be disclosed in the present.[32]

So the historical Christ and the redeeming Christ are no longer the same. The historical Christ was a man. The redeeming Christ is an ongoing messianic-liberating principle, revealed in a new humanity where issues of gender difference or male-female distinctions are no longer relevant.

Two related questions stay in mind when trying to understand where Ruether is now. The first is whether she can justifiably be called a theist. Daphne Hampson thinks not:

> It seems to me questionable that Ruether herself is theistic. . . . In fact, if one reads her work carefully, one notices that she never speaks of God, but rather of people's concept of God, which may lead them on in their striving for justice.[33]

The second question is whether Ruether is on an inevitable journey into the relativism of postmodernity and, indeed, so far down the road that it no longer matters to her whether any metanarrative is true or not. She may well be. For if women's experience is ultimately all we need to deconstruct reality, what we reconstruct in its place is a matter of personal preference, not committed belief.

Postmodernity in Theology and Gender

Most postmodern feminists are no longer engaged in feminist theology from within the Church. The key players have left. Yet, ironically, they then walked out as a modernist, rather

---

[32] Reuther, *Sexism and God-Talk*, p. 131.
[33] Daphne Hampson, *Theology and Feminism* (Oxford: Blackwell, 1990) p. 29.

than a postmodern gesture. Mary Daly left Christianity more than twenty-five years ago, claiming:

> We cannot really belong to institutional religion as it exists. It isn't good enough to be token preachers. It isn't good enough to have our energies drained and co-opted. Singing sexist hymns, praying to a male god breaks our spirit, makes us less than human. The crushing weight of this tradition, of this power structure tells us that *we do not even exist.*[34]

Daphne Hampson similarly shook the dust off her feet, arguing that she could not give assent to the fundamental belief system of the Christian faith. She recognized that Christianity is based on the belief that there is a reality beyond our experience, and the author of that reality is God. For her, a commitment to Christianity entails an acceptance of this metanarrative. Yet she believes it to be untrue, and that it can be seen to be untrue in its practices. She rejects it and therefore is not a Christian. A departure was for both Mary Daly and Daphne Hampson a matter of integrity. They did not agree with the foundation or the practice so they felt they had to go. These reactions were themselves in keeping with modernity. The appeal was still to a framework of truth: the stand was for one metanarrative over another.

It was not until she was well out of the Christian faith that Mary Daly's work took on the distinct postmodern nuance it has today. Yet what is interesting now is that postmodern unbelievers do not usually leave the Church, whether they are men or women, especially if they are receiving a salary. Why should they? If there are no metanarratives anyway, then it matters little whether one stays or goes. One is free to choose one's own style and option. Since not only gender, but also God, is only a linguistic construct (reinforced by practices and rituals) we are free to construct or deconstruct when and where we will. Belief is simply choice of style or preference.

Postmodern feminist theology does more than focus on difference. It uses difference in its deconstruction of 'God'.

---

[34] Mary Daly, 'Exodus Sermon' preached at Boston College in the early 1970s.

One earlier route was through the 'emancipation' of the goddess. Many argued that the goddess has always been there, hidden from view in most of the world's institutional religions, and overlaid by centuries of male thinking. That is why throughout the history of religion she has frequently 'appeared' in various forms and guises. In Catholicism, for example, she comes in the form of the Virgin, and in building statues and shrines to Mary and receiving miracles from the hand of Mary, we are implicitly recognizing her divinity. But beneath this Virgin Mother who has been captured and domesticated by the Catholic Church, is none other than the embodiment of the fundamental religious female principle which undergirds the whole of reality. The pre-moderns were right to fear women, because the female principle is a powerful, cosmic force which, once freed, heralds in a new era for women.

Others argue in a similar way for the 'Christa', the female representation of Christ, who, more truly than the man epitomises the sacrifice that is made for the sins of the world. Women have suffered the sins of sexism and male violence and oppression, they have indeed given their bodies to be broken. Others argue for 'Sophia', the Wisdom of God as the divine eternal feminine principle. Christianity unfolds the cloths which have hidden the God in feminine form and she is released as the Spirit of Wisdom and Truth.

The reason for the interest in the goddess was initially as a reversal of the 'male God' present in Christianity through the ages because the God of Christian tradition is alleged to be *fundamentally* male, not only in name, but in all his attributes. Daphne Hampson sees this 'God' as a projection of the western male psyche, and he therefore incorporates all the characteristics of power, supremacy, authority, divine-rightness and self-sufficiency prized by men. She described the reaction of one of her students on recognizing that the Christian understanding of God incorporated what she disliked most in human beings: 'Now I understand why I have no use for such a god.' For some feminists the way forward was to rediscover god(dess) as the One who gives our experiences meaning.

Most postmoden writers, however, resist the 'reification' of the goddess. To embrace difference does not mean replacing the male 'God-Father' with the female Goddess-Mother. It means deconstructing god altogether. Consequently, in *Beyond God the Father*, Mary Daly not only rejects the idea that women need some 'male divinity and his son' to save them, she also discards 'God' as the name of any deity, personal or impersonal. It makes little actual difference that this god has feminine gender, inclusive gender, or no gender, for the process of deconstruction is not complete until we realize that 'God' is not a noun at all. God is a verb: active, dynamic, moving. God is not Being, but be-ing, the 'I am' of women coming into their own authentic liberation. In the 'original reintroduction' to the volume, written for the second edition ten years later, she attempts to explain the consequences of not sufficiently deconstructing god:

> Naming Be-ing as Verb is an essential leap in the cognitive/ affective journey beyond patriarchal fixations. Serious and unac- knowledged difficulties can arise when those who speak and/or write of the Goddess of goddesses avoid the giant step/leap of Realizing ultimate/intimate reality as movement, as Verb. One result, though unintended is complicity in Verbicide-killing of the living, transforming energy of words, muting of the metamorphic, shape-shifting power inherent in words. Thus, The Goddess can be reduced to a static symbol, a mere replacement for the noun God.[35]

It is only in participation with the Verb that women can be 'saved' because the salvation they need is salvation from sexism, for women are the innocents. Salvation is liberation, freedom to be powerful and released so that:

> Raging/Racing women become Counterclock-Wise, asking Counterclock-Whys. Boundary-shifting Sibyls become Other- Wise, uttering Other Whys. Our very being vibrates with earth, air, fire, water, and with the moon, sun and farthest stars.[36]

---

[35] Mary Daly, 'Original Reintroduction' in *Beyond God the Father* (London: Women's Press, 1986) p. xvii.
[36] ibid. p. xxii.

In both her concepts and presentation, Mary Daly aims indeed to go beyond the bounds of patriarchal religion, deconstructing every aspect of the language in which this religion is expressed. The goal is a dynamic exchange where all that has been influenced by male thought-forms, including, most particularly, words themselves, are re-done: re-employed in a new re-presentation of woman. Perhaps not surprisingly, however, this is regarded by some as obscurantist, smacking again of the elitism and 'self-indulgence' which they see as characteristic of much postmodern feminism. Daly faces the accusation, like Irigaray, of being out of touch and uninterested in women's real battles, especially in non-white, postcolonial cultures. Her later books continue the attempt for this perpetual redoing of our language, beyond patriarchy.

Mary Daly is long gone from the Church. But Carter Heyward is still in it. Yet her deconstruction of 'god', and her use of god-as-verb is no less radical than Mary Daly's. She imagines Christa, not as reified goddess, but as the spirit and process in a woman's lovemaking. In a curious reversal of the pre-modern position, she echoes the idea that women do have a different spiritual identity, closely tied to their sexuality. Yet that difference is not for men to define. Women must claim it for themselves in lesbian sexuality. For god becomes the verb 'to god', and it is in 'godding', especially in 'sexual godding' that women experience their authentic identity most fully. In one passage she describes a passionate lovemaking between women in terms that evoke and fuse it with the eucharist:

> There is no greater delight than to celebrate and share the body of Christa as eternal resource of nourishment on the sacred journey towards justice. I praise her as both ground and figure of our lovemaking. She is in the power between us, in our relation as well as in the persons we are and are becoming, you and I together. I see her in you and I enjoy her in myself. I take her and stroke her playfully. I look upon her with immense tenderness. I take her and nibble a little, I take her and eat, take her and drink. I am taken, grasped, and caressed by her power moving between us. Immersing myself in you, with you, through you, I move with you

in the sensual wellspring of her love. I move with you in the turbulence of her passion.[37]

Not only are our gender and sexuality constructed, to be reconstructed along lines of openness and love, god can similarly be reconstructed as the process through which this openness takes place. Carter Heyward (like Mary Daly) still finds in this process a basis for ethics. But there is no way any critique she offers can be binding on others, because others' experiences might be different, and their processes of deconstruction might have quite a different shape. At most, postmodern feminist theology can only assemble pastiches of ideas, morality and meanings. Beyond that there is little to be said.

Summary

Feminist theology is more than a reaction against the essentialism of a pre-modern attitude. It is also against the abuses of a religion which has sometimes used its authority to deny both full humanity and dignity to women. In that sense its origins in the 'Second Wave' are similar to the origins of secular feminism. Its concerns for a new interpretation of the structures of our lives committed to equality and justice also parallel the concerns of modernist feminists in all other spheres. Similarly, postmodern feminist theology parallels so many of the moves made by other postmodern feminists, with an identical interest in deconstruction and experience-based analyses of reality.

Yet in far more ways feminist theology is not the same as secular feminism, for in asking the same implicit questions about the nature of reality, sexuality, gender and of human personhood, it has still done so, initially at least, from within the Christian faith system. The responses which it produces are diverse because the underlying beliefs begin to shift and diverge. But there is no 'slippery slope'. There is no truth in the

---

[37] Carter Heyward, *Touching Our Strength: The Erotic as Power and the Love of God* (San Francisco: Harper, 1989) pp. 117–8.

accusation that when we start with the biblical examination of Catherine Kroeger or Gretchen Gabelein Hull[38] we end up with the relativism of Mary Daly. The two are in different worlds. And ultimately at the heart of the difference is the growing contrast between faith and unbelief.

---

[38] Richard and Catherine C. Kroeger, *I Suffer Not a Woman: Rethinking 1 Timothy 2:11–15 in the Light of Ancient Evidence* (Grand Rapids: Baker Book House, 1992). Catherine is the president of Christians for Biblical Equality. Gretchen Gabelein Hull is the editor of the 'Priscialla Papers' and author of *Equal to Serve* (London: Scripture Union, 1992).

Chapter Eight

Post-postmodern Postscript

The question of the origin and meaning of human sexuality is obviously important. But what we take as our starting point is vital. In trying to work through one key question in the sex and gender debate I have had to cover much terrain, and using Goux's categories of pre-modern, modern and postmodern has helped me to give some shape to the enquiry, and to look at different starting points. I now want to draft out some responses from a Christian perspective.

Pre-modern, modern and postmodern revisited

It has been clear that each of the positions I have looked at incorporates some important insights, whilst leaving itself open to considerable weaknesses. Pre-modernity acknowledges the givenness of reality, including human reality. It claims that there is something within us and beyond us which structures how we live; something which others, Jean Paul Sartre, for example, vehemently denied: 'There is no human nature, since there is no God to conceive it.'[1] It also believes that there is truth, and we live in a universe where, if some things are true, then their opposites are false. In its Christian form it acknowledges that the world is far bigger than human experience and human life is to be lived before the God who is there. Some Christians have argued too that a pre-modern

---

[1] Jean Paul Sartre, *Existentialism and Humanism* (trans. Philip Mairet; London: Methuen, 1948) p. 28.

perspective can provide some useful tools, especially if an essentialist identity can be seen as a 'representative metaphor entailing human agency and practice, rather than a realist retreat into a nature against which human beings are powerless'.[2]

But there are also some fundamental weaknesses in this position. For without the above qualification, pre-modernity has a reductionist mentality: it takes one thing in creation and makes it an absolute, whether that key thing is biology, maleness, reason or authority. Once anything is made absolute (i.e. becomes 'essentialist'), then the rest of reality is interpreted from that standpoint, with inevitable results. Reality is distorted, the richness and variety of creation is shrunk and the facts are now re-presented to fit the assumptions. What is more, we have a limited basis for our ethics, especially our gender ethics. If we begin with some 'natural' evolutionary framework because it suits our assumptions, we have to recognize that the only shape to our relationships is given ultimately by instinct and drive. But we are much more complex creatures than that. We have emotions, longings, fears, hopes, ambitions, all of which are related to our family attitudes, our moral ideas and our belief system. Furthermore, if we begin from some authoritarian basis in 'male headship' then women's moral responses are ultimately reduced to being about whether they are obedient or disobedient to male structures. Yet, when we take biblical revelation seriously we are given a perspective that suggests we are all equally purposeful, responsible beings who have choices before God about the way we act.

The modern perspective also incorporates vital insights. The attack on reductionism, especially biological reductionism, opens up reality again, and leaves space for the important interplay between 'nature' and 'culture'. This gives us a much stronger basis for ethics, for it recognizes we are moral human beings with ethical choices. It also makes it possible for us to develop concepts of justice and injustice, equality, responsibility for our actions and for other people. However, modernity

---

[2] Graham, *Making the Difference*, p. 190.

has its own grave weaknesses. It has a basic separation of knowledge from faith, which fails to see that knowledge itself is the outworking of faith commitments. In trying to establish a basis for knowing through the primacy of 'women's experience, modernist feminism (and especially feminist theology) fails to recognize that they are making a faith commitment. For underlying its own position is a view of the person as autonomous and a view of knowledge as ultimately subjective. Ultimately, modernity has irreversible internal weaknesses, for it 'relies on precisely that mode of thought that is responsible for the situation it wishes to change'.[3]

Finally, postmodernity incorporates an important critique of modernity. It lays bare the assumptions in its position and looks at the arbitrariness of its definitions, when there is no basis from which to make them. What is 'justice' other than rich people being able to buy expensive lawyers to get them off crimes that everyone knows they have committed? And what is 'gender equality' other than the widening of the goalposts so that women can score the same goals as men? In its refutation of androgyny, it again raises key issues about difference. It sketches some of the important multiple ways our identities are shaped and formed. It also pushes the 'gender construction' argument to its logical conclusion, where there are no demarcations between what is structured and what is not.

The weaknesses of postmodernity are always its relativism. We always have to ask: Where do we deconstruct from? What is our starting point? And since postmodernity has no foundational starting point, it has always to deconstruct from a position of deconstruction, and when constructs are relativised it is from a position of relativism. But this leaves a huge internal problem with the very formulation of a postmodern position. For, what does it mean to say: 'Everything is relative'? What status does this statement have? If it has a merely relative status it cannot be in any sense binding, for it is not actually saying anything. But if 'everything is

---

[3] Francis Martin, *The Feminist Question: Feminist Theology in the Light of Christian Tradition* (Edinburgh: T. & T. Clark, 1994) p. 165.

relative' has an absolute status, then it negates its own formulation. Yet, though the claim to relativism cannot be articulated, it still tries to be prescriptive. It continues to insist that nothing is fixed, and we may not make categorical statements. In fact, relativism at best makes indifference an absolute.

The categories of pre-modern, modern and postmodern have not given us fine details or delineation, but they have given us the shape of the landscape and drawn out the patterns and clusters for us to observe. In trying to make my own response I could argue that a Christian perspective in some ways incorporates elements of all three positions, and this would be a reasonable observation. Elaine Graham, in her chapter on a way forward, outlines a call for a 'constructed essentialism, one which has recourse to a notion of fixed coherent identity, but only as a strategic and enacted category'.[4] This would be an interesting programme to develop. But I could also say that the time has come for me to leave these categories behind. They have done a useful job, but they have their limitations. They are adequate for a rough sketch, but far too vague and nebulous if we are trying to copy a masterpiece.

Some Christian Responses

As an alternative strategy, I want to start by offering another 'Archimedean point' which, as we saw earlier, is a 'place' from which we can survey reality, get an outlook on the world. A perspective that would try to be faithful to the historic Christian faith would begin from a different Archimedean point from either biology, culture or experience. It would start from the acceptance that there is a God, and a world of which we are part. The God who is there is the God whom the Christian Scriptures, in an unfolding revelation, reveal to us: a God who is relational, a God whose name is love, a God who is interpersonal, and involved with the creation. This creating God is one who sets boundaries and breathes morality into the

---

[4] Graham, *Making the Difference*, p. 190.

creation, and who constantly offers us the opportunity to change our lives for the better What is more, God is expressed uniquely and personally in Jesus Christ to whom the Scriptures and the Church bear witness. Christ, in union with the whole Godhead, is the one who has given his life for ours, who offers the power of the Spirit to those who ask, who shows a new kind of authority and breaks down barriers between people. Our 'credal' starting point would also have a commitment to the Bible, not simply for its narrative history or theological teachings, but because it discloses who God is and who we are; it unlocks the truth of God for us. But the Bible has to be understood aright, which involves us in also recognizing that we might get it wrong because our experience is not the primary exegetical hermeneutic. Rather, the Bible contains its own hermeneutical tools; it holds the truth to its own meaning and interpretation.

From this perspective, many things follow. To start with, we can accept that our sexuality is indeed 'given', part of the rich created structure of our humanness. The differences in our sexual make-up are part of the rich complementarity which God has breathed into creation. Yet a creational perspective is different from a 'natural'one; sexuality is not simply that which defines our 'nature'. Creation is ordered, not by something people used to call the 'laws of nature' but by complex normative structures which define and delineate our various relationships. For example, we are not to murder, or to commit adultery; we are to love our neighbours as ourselves; we are not to steal or violate one another. God has regulated the structure of reality, breathed an ethical order into it, and that has implications for our sexuality. Far from being driven by the unremitting desire to procreate, we are given responsibility to use our sexuality wisely and to act always in love. How we express our sexuality matters, and we remain accountable to God.

This is all relevant in our contemporary context. We live in a culture that is highly sexualised and which suggests that because we are sexual people, sexual activity is essential in order for us to be fully actualised content human beings. So the idea that there are boundaries around our sexuality is not a popular one. Yet pre-modernity, modernity or postmodernity have not given us adequate ways of thinking through what it means to be sexual beings, for to be sexual means neither that we are driven to procreate, nor that we have an autonomous, unfettered choice to create our own sexual nuances or express our sexual preferences. It means that our sexuality is the dimension through which we experience our lives and what is important from a Christian perspective is that we find appropriate sexual expressions for the relationships within which we live. Sexuality in friendship is different from that in marriage, or in family relationships, or neighbourhoods or fellowship. When we confuse the integrity of each relationship we lose something crucial.

The distinction between sex and gender is also important, because it helps to avoid the temptation to reduce everything to sex. Yet I think it would be a mistake to think too rigidly of sex as creational and gender as cultural. This suggests too big a dichotomy, that we accept our sex as a creation of God, but we create our gender for ourselves, according to social variants. In fact, if we believe in a God who has given a normative structure to relationships, we have to believe in a God who is as interested in our gender as in our biology. For the way we shape our gender is also part of our human response before God. And so we do need to address issues of power, discrimination, poor communication, injustice, unfaithfulness, violation, competitiveness and stereotypes, because in all of these areas we can contravene the principles which God has given us for gender relationships. We need to develop loving, just, impartial, faithful and open ways of relating with one another, for then we are responding together to the God who is love, justice, righteousness, faithfulness and truth. God calls us into responsible and right relationships, and gender patterns call from us a response of obedience.

We need, therefore, to resist the crippling stereotypes whether they are racial or gender or whatever else, and we need also to recognize that despite popular exhortations, the Bible does not say a great deal about being masculine for God or feminine for Jesus! So many of the stereotypes which proliferate in 'Christian' literature are far from biblical. In fact, the New Testament does not tell us how to be feminine or masculine at all. It offers us one set of characteristics as a guideline for both sexes, the 'fruit of the Spirit': love, joy, peace, patience, kindness, goodness, faithfulness, gentleness and self-control. The fact that these are often interpreted as 'feminine characteristics' ought to set us thinking . . .

Four Paradigms

When we ask of the Bible how the relationship between male and female is to be understood, we do not get one (essentialist) answer. The reply does not focus exclusively on either our biological differences, our gender demarcations, our different experiences or our androgyny. In fact a biblical narrative and analysis of male-female relations is very complex. It is possible to detect four different underlying paradigms which are used interchangeably to describe the relationship between us.

The first is indeed *difference*. In the Genesis story of creation, as well as in many of the narratives about sin, the idea of difference is regularly rehearsed. Eve is not the same as Adam. She is *'ishâ* to his *'îsh*. Man and woman are different in terms of procreation. They also first faced temptation differently: she gave in when she was alone; he, when he was in the company of his wife. They received different penalties as a result of the Fall: the woman in childbearing and the man in husbandry. And throughout the scriptures woman and man are described differently. Women are the 'weaker sex', says Peter, as indeed they were with the restrictions of a patriarchal society. They have different spheres of influence (although these change, as the eulogy to the woman in Proverbs 31 reminds us). There were different gender roles amongst the women and men around Jesus (the women, for example, were the ones who came to anoint his body). Paul suggests different dress codes for men and women at worship and he restrains women in some churches from exercising certain forms of leadership.

Yet difference does not exhaust the biblical perspective. The Bible also incorporates the idea of *sameness*, or *similarity*, when looking at the relationship between women and men.

Again in the creation story, when the first man awoke from his sleep and saw the first woman, his cry was one of recognition, of sameness: 'Here at last is bone of my bone, flesh of my flesh.' At one level the Bible does recognize an element of androgyny in male-female relations. They are both an equal part of the human race. Men and women are more like each other than they are like anything else in creation. So, they are given the same commands to be fruitful and multiply, to replenish the earth. They are given the same status over the rest of creation, the same responsibility for procreation. Children too are given the same command with regard to both mother and father: that they are to respect and obey their parents. Men and women are given the same moral requirements, the same mandate against idolatry, the same requirement for faithfulness to God. In their marital sexuality, they are to have the same freedoms and constraints. What is more, within the Church they have the same gifting. The prophet. Joel foresaw the time when God would pour out his spirit on all flesh, where sons and daughters would prophesy. And in the New Testament Church the gifts were given generously, and indiscriminately, to women and men. Most of all, Paul reminds us that in Christ the dividing concepts of 'male' and 'female' are no longer appropriate (Galatians 3:28). In Christ we are all one, and after death there will be no marriage, which seems to mean that our sameness as part of the human creation will go with us into the next world.

The third category is *complementarity*. It is not that women and men are simply the same or different from each other; they are also complementary. That means they 'fit' together, they each reciprocate and fulfil something in the other. The first man was not complemented by any of the animals that he had named. They were fundamentally different from him. The woman complemented him. In one of his letters to the church at Corinth, St Paul talks about the complementary nature of woman and man. In Christ woman is not independent of man, nor is man independent of woman. Just as woman came from man, now man comes from woman (1 Corinthians 11:11). Complementarity does not imply hierarchy, however, as many have taken it to imply. It is premised on the reciprocation and completion of female by male and male by female.

Finally, the Bible also indicates the importance of *union*. Women and men are together as the image of God. The story of creation of man and woman stresses their 'ontological union' more than anything else. For the man was made as distinct from the animals, from the 'dust of the earth', as a separate creation. But when Genesis tells the story of the woman's creation, God did not return to the clay to remodel a second being. Instead, out of the form of the first human, there were now two. Women and men are not ontologically different, with different spiritual identities, but are in union as humankind. This union is followed right through Scripture. There is a union of disobedience, a union of redemption. Both the author of Genesis and St Paul offer us a picture of union of male and female in marriage where they are once again 'one flesh.' St Paul tells us that husband and wife no longer even have ownership of their own bodies. The husband has 'authority' over his wife's sexuality; the wife has 'authority' over her husband's. This is not to encourage possessiveness or abuse, but so that we can know something about the union of love within our humanness. Metaphors for our unity abound in the New Testament: as the Church, we are together the 'body' of Christ, and we are together the 'bride' of Christ. We are the 'living stones' the 'royal priesthood' together. Our deepest experiences, both physical and spiritual, are not of autonomy, difference or separateness, but of the unity of male and female in God.

When we fail to grasp that the Bible holds together each of these themes, we inevitably distort the full biblical message. In turn, that distorts our theology and it leads to vehement reactions and repudiations. If we focus only on one say difference or complementarity as the biblical perspective, then we distort the male-female relationship and inevitably end up with hierarchy and subordination. If we focus on another for example sameness, we again distort the full biblical picture, and reinforce androgyny and lose the significance of our differences. Butwhen we work with all four, then we see the sweep of the biblical revelation and the space and scope it gives to us to develop our relationships faithfully and creatively.

The Gospel as a Deconstruction

That is why we do not need to be afraid of deconstruction, once we have the basis from which to do that. The biblical revelation actually offers a foundation from which we may contextualise the gender relationships which have developed in our societies and understand them better. The New Testament shows us how Jesus himself contextualised gender relations, sometimes stripping away centuries of patriarchal distortions. Take the Samaritan woman at the well of Sychar (John 4). The construction of race and gender in that society meant that communication between Jesus and the woman would have been taboo. Especially, his request for a drink of water transgressed the sexual, gender, race and religious codes that he, as a Jewish male, was required to observe. It is interesting that as a result of the conversation that follows these cultural violations she is recorded as becoming the first evangelist. In another story – the account of the woman with menstrual problems (Luke 8:43–48) – we see another example of how Jesus relativises gender constructions, in this case, constructions of what is clean or unclean and acceptable or unacceptable behaviour for a woman. In this incident, when Jesus's clothing had been touched by a menstruating women, the 'normal' response would have been for Jesus to have seriously rebuked her for having contaminated him, making him unclean and then to have left the crowd to go through the required ablutions. Instead, he stays where he is, brings healing to the woman and re-interprets what she has done. He tells her to go in peace and commends her faith and initiative. Similar 'deconstructions' of the meaning given to women is recorded in the stories of Mary and Martha, of the Cyro-Phoenician woman, of the widow who gives her mite to the offering and the woman who anointed Jesus.

The fundamental question is: From what basis do we try to understand what it means to be a human male or female, and how we should express those differences in our relationships? My argument in this final chapter is that we cannot start from within a pre-modern, modern or postmodern position. The problem is that because the Bible has been dismissed from most of scholarship since the Enlightenment, our culture has been robbed of a powerful basis for beginning again to grasp the meaning of human personhood. When we once more take seriously the rich broad sweep of biblical literature, we are confronted with key themes which have travelled through the centuries and help today to make sense of our relationships with each other. The narratives of creation, sin and redemption offer us an alternative journey to that which our culture has been making. They give us a cogent framework for putting together the story of our humanness and our identity. Sexuality and gender are a crucial part of that story, as we see the damage that has been done to women and men alike, and the distortions that still pervert our relationships and societal structures. But we do not see things aright by elevating our own autonomous experience, or by walking down a deadend into relativism. The uniqueness of the biblical alternative is that the answer to the brokenness of the past, or present, does not lie ultimately with us at all. It is in the Gospel of Christ that all things can be made anew.

Further Reading

Sex, Gender and Theory

Altman, Dennis, et al. (eds.), *Homosexuality, Which Homosexuality?: International Conference on Gay and Lesbian Studies* (London: GMO Publishers, 1989)

Butler, J., *Gender Trouble: Feminism and the Subversion of Identity* (New York: Routledge, 1990)

Brandotti, R., 'The Ethics of Sexual Difference: The Case of Foucault and Irigaray' *Australian Feminist Studies* (1986)

——, *Patterns of Dissonance: A study of Women in Contemporary Philosophy*, trans. Elizabeth Guild (Cambridge: Polity, 1991)

Brown, A., *The Darwin Wars: How Stupid Genes Became Selfish Gods* (London: Simon and Schuster, 1999)

Foucault, Michel, *The History of Sexuality*, 2 vols. (Harmondsworth: Penguin 1981, 1987)

Fuss, Diana, *Essentially Speaking: Feminism, Nature and Difference* (New York: Routledge, 1989)

——, *Inside/Out: Lesbian Theories, Gay Theories* (New York: Routledge, 1991)

Goux, Jean Joseph, *Symbolic Economies* (Ithaca: Cornell University Press, 1990)

Gunew, S., *Feminism: Critique and Construct* (London: Routledge, 1992)

Lacan, Jacques, *The Four Fundamental Concepts of Psychoanalysis*, Jacques Alain Miller (ed.), trans. Alan Sheridan (New York: Norton, 1978)

——, 'God and the Jousisance' in *Feminine Spirituality: Jacques Lacan and the Ecole Fruedienne*, trans J. Rose (New York: Norton, 1983)

MacCannel, J.F., *Figuring Lacan: Criticism and the Cultural Consciousness* (New York: Routledge, 1986)

Storkey, Alan, *Foundational Epistemologies in Consumption Theory* (Amsterdam: Free University Press, 1993)

Sex, Gender and Society

Arber, S. and J. Ginn, *Gender and Later Life: A Sociological Analysis of Resources and Constraints* (London: Sage, 1991)

Arnot, M. and K. Weiler, *Feminism and Social Justice in Education* (London: Falmer Press, 1993)

Deem, R., *Women and Schooling* (London: Routledge, 1978)

Dex, Shirley, *The Sexual Division of Work* (Hemel Hempstead: Harvester Wheatsheaf, 1985)

——, *Women's Occupational Mobility: A Lifetime Perspective* (London: Macmillan, 1987)

Glendinning, C. and J. Millar, *Women and Poverty in Britain* (Hemel Hempstead: Harvester, Wheatsheaf, 1992)

Greer, Germaine, *Sex and Destiny: The Politics of Human Fertility* (New York: Harper & Row, 1984)

Hallett, Christine (ed), *Women and Social Policy: An Introduction* (London: Prentice Hall, 1996)

Hooks, Bell, *Yearning: Race, Gender and Cultural Politics* (Boston: South End Press, 1990)

Phillips, A., 'Feminism, Equality and Difference' in Linda McDowell, and Rosemary Pringle (eds.) *Defining Women: Social Institutions and Gender Divisions* (Cambridge: Polity Press, 1992)

Roberts, M., *Living in a Man-made World: Gender Assumptions in Modern Housing Design* (London: Routledge, 1991)

Segal, L., *Is the Future Female? Troubled Thoughts on Contemporary Feminism* (London: Virago, 1987)

Shalit, Wendy, *A Return to Modesty: Discovering the Lost Virtue* (London: Simon and Schuster, 1999)

Smith, L.T., 'Maori Women, Education and the Struggles for Mana Wahine' in M. Arnot and K. Weiler (eds) *Feminism and Social Justice in Education* (London: Falmer Press, 1993)

Waring, Marilyn, *If Women Counted: A New Feminist Economics* (London: McMillan, 1988)

Weeks, Jeffrey, *Sex. Politics and Society* (London: Longmans, 1981)

Wellings, K., et al., *Sexual Behaviour in Britain: The National Survey of Sexual Attitudes and Lifestyles* (Harmondsworth: Penguin, 1995)

Whitelegg, Marilyn, et al., *The Changing Experience of Women* (Oxford: Martin Robertson, 1982)

Marriage and Family

Atkinson, David, *To Have and to Hold* (London: Collins, 1979)

Dominion, Jack, *Marriage: The Definitive Guide to What Makes a Marriage Work* (London: Heinemann, 1995)

Friday, Nancy, *My Mother My Self* (London: Fontana, 1977)

Fukuyama, F., *The Great Disruption: Human Nature and the Reconstitution of Social Order* (London: Profile Books, 1999)

Hite, Shere, *The Hite Report on the Family: Growing Up Under Patriarchy* (London: Bloomsbury 1995)

Oakley, Ann, *From Here to Maternity* (Harmondsworth: Penguin, 1981)

Storkey, Alan, *Marriage and its Modern Crisis: Repairing Married Life* (London: Hodder & Stoughton, 1996)

Torrance, D.W., *God, Family and Sexuality* (Carberry: The Handsel Press, 1997)

Masculinity

Bly, R., *Iron John: A Book About Men* (Reading, Mass: Addison-Wesley, 1990)

Doty, W., *Myths of Masculinity* (New York: Crossroad, 1993)

Farrell, W., *The Myth of Male Power* (New York: Random House, 1994)

Hollis, J., *Under Saturn's Shadow* (Toronto: Inner City Books, 1989)

McCloughry, Roy, *Men and Masculinity* (London: Hodder & Stoughton, 1992)

O'Connor, Peter, *The Inner Man* (Sydney: Macmillan, 1992)
Tatham, Peter, *The Makings of Maleness* (London: Karnac Books, 1992)

Violence and Gender

Barron, J., *Not Worth the Paper...? The Effectiveness of Legal Protection for Women and Children Experiencing Domestic Violence* (Bristol: WAFE, 1990)
Bhavnaani, K.K., 'Is Violence Masculine?' in Shabnam Grewal et al (eds.) *Charting the Journey: Writings by Black and Third World Women* (London: Sheba, 1990)
Hooper, Carol-Ann, *Mothers Surviving Child Sexual Abuse* (London: Routledge, 1992)
Newman, Rebecca, *Releasing the Scream* (London: Hodder & Stoughton, 1994)
Radford, J. and D. Russell (eds), *Femicide: The Politics of Woman Killing* (Buckingham: Open University Press, 1992)

Sex, Gender and Theology

Bilezikian, Gilbert, *Beyond Sex Roles: What the Bible Says About a Woman's Place in Church and Family* (Grand Rapids: Baker Book House, 1986)
Evans, Mary J., *Woman in the Bible* (Exeter: Paternoster, 1984)
Groothuis, R., *Good News For Women: A Biblical Picture of Gender Equality* (Grand Rapids: Baker Books, 1997)
Hebblethwaite, Margaret, *Motherhood and God* (London: Geoffrey Chapman, 1984)
Hebblethwaite, Margaret and Elaine Storkey, *Conversations on Christian Feminism* (London: HarperCollins, 1999)
Hull, Gretchen Gaebelein, *Equal to Serve: Women and Men in the Church and Home* (New Jersey: Fleming H. Revell, 1987)
King, Ursula, *Faith and Praxis in a Postmodern Age* (London: Cassell, 1998)
Kroeger, Catherine Clark, Mary J. Evans and Elaine Storkey, *The Women's Study New Testament: Based on the NRSV* (London: Marshall Pickering / Grand Rapids: Baker Book House, 1995)

ttauer, Florence, *Wake Up, Women! Submission Doesn't Mean Stupidity* (Dallas: Word Publishing, 1994)

Lorde, A. 'An Open Letter to Mary Daly' in *Sister Outsider* (New York: Crossing Press, 1984)

Malcolm, K.T., *Women at the Crossroads: A Path Beyond Feminism and Traditionalism* (Downers Grove: Inter-Varsity Press, 1982)

Martin, Faith, *Call Me Blessed* (Grand Rapids: Eerdmans, 1988)

Mbuga, Judy, *Our Time Has Come: African Christian Women Address the Issues of Today* (Carlisle: Paternoster, 1994)

Mickelsen, Alvera (ed), *Women, Authority and the Bible* (Downers Grove: InterVaristy Press, 1986)

Moltmann-Wendel, Elisabeth and Jürgen Moltmann, *God: His and Hers* (London: SCM, 1991)

Perriman, Andrew, *Speaking of Women: Interpreting Paul* (London: Apollos, 1998)

Reid, John, Lesslie Newbigin and David L. Pullinger, *Modern, Postmodern and Christian* (Carberry: Handsel Press, 1997)

Ruether, Rosemary Radford, *New Woman New Earth: Sexist Ideologies and Human Liberation* (New York: The Seabury Press, 1975)

——, *To Change the World: Christology and Cultural Criticism* (New York: Crossroad, 1981)

Storkey, Alan, *The Meanings of Love* (Leicester: IVP, 1994)

Storkey, Elaine, *Contributions to Christian Feminsm* (London: Impact Publications, 1995)

——, *Magnify the Lord* (London: HarperCollins, 1997)

Stott, John, *New Issues Facing Christians Today* (London: Marshall Pickering, 1999)

Torrance, T.F., *The Ministrsy of Women* (Carberry: Handsel Press, 1992)

West, A., *Deadly Innocence: Feminism and the Mythology of Sin* (London: Cassell, 1995)

Author Index

Subject Index